D1736657

INTRODUCING
ISSUES WITH
OPPOSING
VIEWPOINTS®

Fast Food

Lauri S. Friedman, *Book Editor*

GREENHAVEN PRESS
A part of Gale, Cengage Learning

GALE
CENGAGE Learning·

Detroit • New York • San Francisco • New Haven, Conn • Waterville, Maine • London

Christine Nasso, *Publisher*
Elizabeth Des Chenes, *Managing Editor*

© 2010 Greenhaven Press, a part of Gale, Cengage Learning

Gale and Greenhaven Press are registered trademarks used herein under license.

For more information, contact:
Greenhaven Press
27500 Drake Rd.
Farmington Hills, MI 48331-3535
Or you can visit our Internet site at gale.cengage.com

Articles in Greenhaven Press anthologies are often edited for length to meet page requirements. In addition, original titles of these works are changed to clearly present the main thesis and to explicitly indicate the author's opinion. Every effort is made to ensure that Greenhaven Press accurately reflects the original intent of the authors. Every effort has been made to trace the owners of copyrighted material.

Cover image copyright LockStockBob, 2010. Used under license from Shutterstock.com.

LIBRARY OF CONGRESS CATALOGING-IN-PUBLICATION DATA
Fast food / Lauri S. Friedman, book editor.
p. cm. -- (Introducing issues with opposing viewpoints)
Includes bibliographical references and index.
ISBN 978-0-7377-4733-1 (hardcover)
1. Obesity--United States--Juvenile literature. 2. Convenience foods--Health aspects--United States--Juvenile literature. 3. Fast food restaurants--Health aspects--United States--Juvenile literature. I. Friedman, Lauri S.
RA645.O23F53 2010
362.196'398--dc22
2009051963

Printed in the United States of America
1 2 3 4 5 6 7 14 13 12 11 10

Contents

Foreword

Indulging in a wide spectrum of ideas, beliefs, and perspectives is a critical cornerstone of democracy. After all, it is often debates over differences of opinion, such as whether to legalize abortion, how to treat prisoners, or when to enact the death penalty, that shape our society and drive it forward. Such diversity of thought is frequently regarded as the hallmark of a healthy and civilized culture. As the Reverend Clifford Schutjer of the First Congregational Church in Mansfield, Ohio, declared in a 2001 sermon, "Surrounding oneself with only like-minded people, restricting what we listen to or read only to what we find agreeable is irresponsible. Refusing to entertain doubts once we make up our minds is a subtle but deadly form of arrogance." With this advice in mind, Introducing Issues with Opposing Viewpoints books aim to open readers' minds to the critically divergent views that comprise our world's most important debates.

Introducing Issues with Opposing Viewpoints simplifies for students the enormous and often overwhelming mass of material now available via print and electronic media. Collected in every volume is an array of opinions that captures the essence of a particular controversy or topic. Introducing Issues with Opposing Viewpoints books embody the spirit of nineteenth-century journalist Charles A. Dana's axiom: "Fight for your opinions, but do not believe that they contain the whole truth, or the only truth." Absorbing such contrasting opinions teaches students to analyze the strength of an argument and compare it to its opposition. From this process readers can inform and strengthen their own opinions, or be exposed to new information that will change their minds. Introducing Issues with Opposing Viewpoints is a mosaic of different voices. The authors are statesmen, pundits, academics, journalists, corporations, and ordinary people who have felt compelled to share their experiences and ideas in a public forum. Their words have been collected from newspapers, journals, books, speeches, interviews, and the Internet, the fastest growing body of opinionated material in the world.

Introducing Issues with Opposing Viewpoints shares many of the well-known features of its critically acclaimed parent series, Opposing Viewpoints. The articles are presented in a pro/con format, allowing readers to absorb divergent perspectives side by side. Active reading questions preface each viewpoint, requiring the student to approach the material thoughtfully and carefully. Useful charts, graphs, and cartoons supplement each article. A thorough introduction provides readers with crucial background on an issue. An annotated bibliography points the reader toward articles, books, and Web sites that contain additional information on the topic. An appendix of organizations to contact contains a wide variety of charities, nonprofit organizations, political groups, and private enterprises that each hold a position on the issue at hand. Finally, a comprehensive index allows readers to locate content quickly and efficiently.

Introducing Issues with Opposing Viewpoints is also significantly different from Opposing Viewpoints. As the series title implies, its presentation will help introduce students to the concept of opposing viewpoints and learn to use this material to aid in critical writing and debate. The series' four-color, accessible format makes the books attractive and inviting to readers of all levels. In addition, each viewpoint has been carefully edited to maximize a reader's understanding of the content. Short but thorough viewpoints capture the essence of an argument. A substantial, thought-provoking essay question placed at the end of each viewpoint asks the student to further investigate the issues raised in the viewpoint, compare and contrast two authors' arguments, or consider how one might go about forming an opinion on the topic at hand. Each viewpoint contains sidebars that include at-a-glance information and handy statistics. A Facts About section located in the back of the book further supplies students with relevant facts and figures.

Following in the tradition of the Opposing Viewpoints series, Greenhaven Press continues to provide readers with invaluable exposure to the controversial issues that shape our world. As John Stuart Mill once wrote: "The only way in which a human being can make some approach to knowing the whole of a subject is by hearing what can be said about it by persons of every variety of opinion and studying all modes in which it can be looked at by every character of mind. No wise man ever acquired his wisdom in any mode but this." It is to this principle that Introducing Issues with Opposing Viewpoints books are dedicated.

Introduction

In the wake of the successful lawsuits against tobacco companies in the 1990s—in which they were found liable, or responsible, for damaging the health of their customers—many have wondered whether fast-food companies might one day be held responsible for harming the health and well-being of American consumers. Whether fast food can or should be treated like tobacco is a heated topic of debate that is likely to be pursued with increasing vigor in upcoming years.

Some argue that fast food is an unhealthy, addictive product that companies like McDonald's and Burger King negligently sell to American customers. They claim fast food is unnecessarily laden with calories and fat and, as such, contributes to high rates of diseases such as diabetes, hypertension, heart attack, stroke, and more. Therefore, opponents of fast food think it should be treated like tobacco and be subject to heavy regulations. This camp has proposed banning fast-food restaurants in high-risk areas, prohibiting fast-food advertising to children, adding a special tax to fast food, and above all, allowing fast-food companies to be sued for knowingly making Americans sick.

Yet thus far, U.S. courts have been reluctant to solidly back any of these claims, indicating that fast food is unlikely to be the next tobacco in the near future. For example, only a handful of lawsuits have been brought against fast-food companies so far, and none have been very successful. One was in August 2002, when two teenage girls filed a lawsuit against McDonald's. The girls claimed that McDonald's failed to warn them that its food was not only unhealthy but also addictive. Almost all of their claims were dismissed, and the remaining ones are still pending further legal motions, with little expectation that the outcome will be significant. The case (known as *Pelman v. McDonald's Corp.*) has been proof for some that trying to make fast-food companies liable for consumers' health will not work as it did with tobacco companies.

Another lawsuit against McDonald's involved the company's failure to disclose that its french fries were made with beef fat. McDonald's settled the matter simply by donating $10 million to charity. The restaurant chain donated another $7 million to the American Heart Association after it was sued for not removing trans fats from its foods after it promised to. Writes lawyer Lianne S. Pinchuk, "The settlements and awards so far in fast food class action litigation don't even begin to compare to the hundreds of millions of dollars in damages awarded to individual plaintiffs in tobacco litigation. And there is little reason to believe that such awards may significantly increase over time."[1]

Pinchuk also reports that as of 2007, twenty-three states had passed laws that protect food companies from being threatened with what are called "obesity lawsuits," or lawsuits in which people allege a company's products made them fat. For example, in 2003 Louisiana passed a law that limited the damages that could be awarded to plaintiffs who claim they have been damaged by eating food and drinking nonalcoholic beverages. Similarly, in Florida, food makers, sellers, and distributors are protected from being found responsible for the poor health, sickness, or death of someone who suffers from a health condition related to obesity.

Protections from these types of lawsuits have been afforded by states mainly because of the idea that fast-food companies do not force people to eat their food—people decide whether they want to eat it and thus are ultimately responsible for their health. Furthermore, the people who frequent fast-food restaurants are both fat and skinny, healthy and unhealthy—this is very different than consumers of tobacco, all of whom eventually develop some level of addiction and decreased health as a result of smoking. Food companies can be sued if they do something clearly wrong, such as lie to their customers about what is in their food or falsely advertise their products. But for the most part, according to Pinchuk, "Fast food companies are enjoying more protections than tobacco companies ever did, and it appears that Big Food is not the next Big Tobacco."[2]

Moreover, while it has been suggested that fast food is addictive, it has been difficult to prove it is as addictive, or addictive in the same way, as cigarettes and other tobacco products. While fast food appeals to some, others find it greasy and indigestible. Furthermore, fast food comes in myriad forms—everything from salad to burgers to wraps to deli sandwiches. These offerings are vastly different from tobacco products, which are made up principally of nicotine and tar and become addictive and harmful to health within a few months or even weeks of use.

Put another way, not everyone who eats fast food will continually crave it—many people will eat it only once in a while, and still others are not tempted at all by fast food. But everyone who smokes cigarettes or other tobacco products will become physically addicted to them at some point, and most smokers do not indulge in the habit occasionally. For these reasons, many argue that fast food cannot be legislated against in the way tobacco has been. "Fast food [is] not 'addictive.' If [it] were, The Ronald McDonald House would be for recovering burger-heads instead of families with terminally ill children," says writer Rachel Heiderscheidt. "Rather, these decisions are a lifestyle, a way we choose to live and care for our bodies. Eating one cheeseburger does not lead to becoming physically and emotionally dependent upon the consumption of them. . . . The choice to continually do either of these things is our own."[3] Many agree with Heiderscheidt, arguing that using the tobacco lawsuits as a model for fast-food lawsuits is not likely to work.

Yet not everyone is convinced. This is why each year, more cities decide to impose regulations on fast-food restaurants, such as requiring them to post the nutritional content of their dishes. Some mayors and other politicians have gotten behind the idea of a "fast-food tax," the proceeds from which would go to offset the cost of treating diabetes and obesity, the same way in which money earned from cigarette taxes is spent on youth–smoking prevention programs and other public initiatives. It is also possible that the coming years might see a lawsuit that finds a way to successfully make fast-food companies liable for their products. In other words, whether fast food will become the next tobacco remains to be seen. This and other issues surrounding fast food—such as whether it can be healthy, and whether regulations should be placed on its advertising—are among the many debates presented in *Introducing Issues with Opposing Viewpoints: Fast Food.* Pro/con article pairs expose readers to the basic debates surrounding fast food and encourage them to develop their own opinions on the topic.

Notes

1. Lianne S. Pinchuk, "Are Fast Food Lawsuits Likely to Be the Next 'Big Tobacco'?" *National Law Journal,* February 28, 2007.

2. Pinchuk, "Are Fast Food Lawsuits Likely to Be the Next 'Big Tobacco'?"

3. Rachel Heiderscheidt, "Fast Food: Not Quite Crack: Over-Eating Is a Lifestyle Choice Rather than a Physical Compulsion," *(Mankato, MN) Reporter,* December 5, 2006. http://media.www.msu reporter.com/media/storage/paper937/news/2006/12/05/Voices/Fast-Food.Not.Quite.Crack-2522702.shtml#4.

Chapter 1

Is Fast Food Bad for You?

Critics attack McDonald's menu for being high in fat, sodium, and calories.

Fast Food Is Unhealthy

Sarah Irani

> *"Containing less fat, salt and sugar, your pet's food may be healthier than what they serve at McDonald's."*

In the following viewpoint Sarah Irani gives multiple reasons that fast food is unhealthy. In addition to being laden with fat and calories, fast food contains high levels of sodium, sugar, and many chemicals, she claims. It also contributes to illnesses such as erectile dysfunction and erodes the tissue that lines blood vessels. She further asserts that fast food is prepared in unsanitary conditions and loaded with so many preservatives that a ten-year-old hamburger will look about the same as a fresh one. Finally, Irani says fast food is not only bad for people, but for the planet—rainforests are cut down to clear land for growing cheap feed for the animals that are slaughtered for fast food. For all of these reasons, Irani recommends avoiding fast food whenever possible.

Irani's articles have appeared on AlterNet .org and EcoSalon.com, where this viewpoint was originally published.

AS YOU READ, CONSIDER THE FOLLOWING QUESTIONS:

1. How long does Irani say a person would have to walk in order to burn off the calories in a supersized Coke, fries, and a Big Mac?

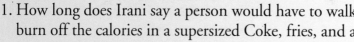

2. What were workers in an Orlando, Florida–area McDonald's caught doing on camera, according to Irani?
3. List at least six ingredients the author says are found in a McDonald's latte.

The Golden Arches: the ultimate American icon. [The documentary] *Super Size Me* taught us that fast food culture brings obesity, heart disease, hypertension and a whole slew of other problems. How bad do you really want that Big Mac? Here are 15 reasons you'll never let anyone you love get near those Golden Arches.

Fast Food Is Heavily Preserved and Full of Fat

Real food is perishable. With time, it begins to decay. It's a natural process, it just happens. Beef will rot, bread will mold. But what about a McDonald's burger? Karen Hanrahan saved a McDonald's burger from 1996 and, oddly enough, it looks just as "appetizing" and "fresh" as a burger you might buy today. Is this real food?

You would have to walk 7 hours straight to burn off a Super Sized Coke, fries and Big Mac. Even indulging in fast food as an occasional treat is a recipe for weight gain . . . unless you're planning to hit each treadmill in the treadmill bay afterwards.

Containing less fat, salt and sugar, your pet's food may be healthier than what they serve at McDonald's.

Fast Food Restaurants Are Not Sanitary

In 2007, the employees of an Orlando [Florida]–area McDonald's were caught on camera pouring milk into the milkshake machine out of a bucket labeled "Soiled Towels Only." That particular restaurant had already been cited for 12 different sanitary violations. Though McDonald's proudly stands by its safety standards, and not every restaurant has such notorious incidents, the setting of a fast food restaurant staffed with low-paid employees at a high turnover rate arguably encourages bending the rules. (McDonald's isn't alone in this, of course—Burger King is actually ranked as the dirtiest of all the fast food chains.)

Fast-Food Calories Add Up

Many fast-food sandwiches contain more than 1,000 calories. When customers add a drink and fries to their order, they go well over their fat, sodium, and sometimes their calorie allowances for an entire day.

Fattest Fast-Food Burgers	Serving Size (g)	Calories	Fat (g)	Sodium (mg)	Carbs (g)	Protein (mg)
BK Double Whopper w/cheese	398	1010	66	1530	52	53
BK Triple Whopper w/cheese	480	1250	84	1600	52	73
Carl's Jr. Original $6 Burger	430	1010	68	1980	60	40
Carl's Jr. Bacon Cheese $6 Burger	409	1070	76	1910	50	46
Hardee's 1/2 lb $6 Burger	412	1060	73	1950	58	40
Hardee's 2/3 lb Double Bacon Cheese Thickburger	409	1300	97	2200	50	54
Hardee's 2/3 lb Monster Thick Burger	424	1420	108	2770	46	60
Jack in the Box Bacon Ultimate Cheeseburger	338	1090	77	2040	53	46
Jack in the Box Ultimate Cheese Burger	323	1010	71	1500	53	40

Fattest fast food burgers under 1,000 calories

	Serving Size (g)	Calories	Fat (g)	Sodium (mg)	Carbs (g)	Protein (mg)
In-N-Out Double Double w/onion	330	670	41	1440	39	37
Fatburger King Burger	400	820	41	1310	64	49
McDonald's Double Quarter Pounder w/cheese	279	740	42	1380	40	48
Super Sonic Cheeseburger w/Mayo	343	980	64	1430	58	46
Wendy's 3/4 lb Triple w/cheese	410	980	60	2010	43	69

Encouraging Antienvironmental Principles

McDonald's supports the destruction of the Amazon rainforest. Much of the soy-based animal feed used to fatten fast-food chickens is grown in the Amazon. Are those chicken nuggets really worth acres of irreplaceable trees? (Especially considering how important carbon sinks like the rainforest are to halt global warming!) Fast food supports a completely unsustainable system of agriculture. It's cruel to animals, unhealthy for humans, and bad for the planet.

Even Prince Charles, while touring a diabetes center in the United Arab Emirates, commented that banning McDonald's is key to health and nutrition. Don't let the salads and chicken breasts fool you. The "chicken" at McDonald's, by the way, comes with a whole lot more than chicken.

As if feeding children high-fat, high-sodium, low-nutrition "food" weren't bad enough, some Happy Meals in 2006 contained toy Hummers. It's as if McDonald's was encouraging a whole generation of kids not only to guzzle food, but to guzzle gas as well. Would you like a few barrels of petroleum with that?

Fast Food Causes Endothelial and Erectile Dysfunction

The processed fat in McDonald's food (and other fast food) promotes endothelial dysfunction for up to 5 hours after eating the meal. Endothelial tissue is what lines the inside of blood vessels.

For those who enjoy sex, take note: erectile dysfunction is connected to endothelial dysfunction. Morgan Spurlock of *Super Size Me* commented that his normally healthy sexual function deteriorated in just one month when he ate only food from McDonald's. Even his girlfriend commented on camera that "he's having a hard time, you know, getting it up."

What Is in Your Food?

How many cows does it take to keep the world loaded with Big Macs? I had to do some research and a little math, but according to a brief video inside one of McDonald's 6 meat processing plants, about 500,000 pounds of beef is processed per day, per plant. If an average beef cow weighs 1,150 pounds, that means 2,609 cows a day are turned into burgers. That's 952,285 cows per year. And that's just in the United

States. Eating a hamburger may not be worse than driving a Hummer, but it's bad. One hamburger patty does not necessarily come from one cow. Think about that. You're eating bits of hundreds of cows.

Laden with Chemicals, Salt, and Beef

Maybe you just pop in for an inexpensive latte. Watch out for the caramel syrup (Sugar, water, fructose, natural (plant source) and artificial flavor, salt, caramel color (with sulfites), potassium sorbate (preservative), citric acid, malic acid) or the chocolate drizzle (Corn syrup, water, hydrogenated coconut oil, high fructose corn syrup, glycerin, nonfat milk, cocoa, cocoa (processed with alkali), food starch-modified, disodium phosphate, potassium sorbate (preservative), xanthan gum, artificial flavor (vanillin), salt, soy lecithin). Please don't put that stuff into your body. Eat healthy cheap food instead—you can be well and still save cash.

Are you a vegetarian with a French fry craving? You better skip McDonald's because their fries actually contain milk (and wheat) and though they're fried in vegetable oil, the oil is flavored with beef extract. (McDonald's famously misled customers for years.)

Do you want high blood pressure? Hit the drive-through. Eating a McDonald's chicken sandwich (any of 'em, take your pick) will give you about 2/3 of the recommended daily amount of sodium. And if you actually do have high blood pressure, that's way more than you really need.

Cheap Food Has High Consequences

Finally unveiled: the secret of the Big Mac's "secret sauce."

Soybean oil, pickle relish [diced pickles, high fructose corn syrup, sugar, vinegar, corn syrup, salt, calcium chloride, xanthan gum, potassium sorbate (preservative), spice extractives, polysorbate 80], distilled vinegar, water, egg yolks, high fructose corn syrup, onion powder, mustard seed, salt, spices, propylene glycol alginate, sodium benzoate (preservative), mustard bran, sugar, garlic powder, vegetable protein (hydrolyzed corn, soy and wheat), caramel color, extractives of paprika, soy lecithin, turmeric (color), calcium disodium EDTA (protect flavor).

A person would have to walk for approximately seven hours to burn off the calories contained in McDonald's supersized Coke, fries, and Big Mac hamburger.

Yum. Cheap oil and cheap syrup. Many people depend upon cheap food such as the sort offered at McDonald's, whether due to the economic conditions we currently face or low incomes. So shouldn't we be examining regulations that subsidize corn syrup but consider fruits and vegetables the building blocks of a healthy body and green planet—to be "speciality" crops? Shouldn't we be promoting urban gardening, community gardens and spreading information about low-cost farmers' markets and CSAs [Community Supported Agriculture]? And focusing on the abundant choices of cheap food that are tasty and green? . . .

Stay in the know about fast food restaurants—McDonald's isn't the only one to avoid.

EVALUATING THE AUTHOR'S ARGUMENTS:

In this viewpoint Sarah Irani uses facts, examples, and details to make her argument that fast food is unhealthy. She does not, however, use any quotations to support her points. If you were to rewrite this article and insert quotations, what authorities might you quote from? Where would you place these quotations to bolster the points Irani makes?

Fast Food Is Not Always Unhealthy

Alex Markels

"Higher-quality ingredients ultimately result in better-tasting food."

Fast food is not always unhealthy, argues Alex Markels in the following viewpoint. He reports on the fast-food chain Chipotle, which is increasingly popular due to its freshly prepared food made with high-quality ingredients. Its meat is free-range and its dairy products do not contain hormones. Chipotle does not serve sweets or cook its food in automated deep-fry machines. Markels says Chipotle's fresh, healthy approach to fast food has helped the company reach new heights of success in recent years and has also helped it prove that fast food does not have to be unhealthy.

Markels is a reporter for *U.S. News & World Report*, in which this viewpoint was originally printed.

AS YOU READ, CONSIDER THE FOLLOWING QUESTIONS:
1. What happened when Chipotle switched to using free-range pork in its *carnitas*?
2. What is Chipotle's "Food with Integrity" initiative, as described by the author?
3. How are Chipotle's kitchens organized, according to Markels? In what way does the kitchen setup indicate a higher-than-normal quality of fast food?

Alex Markels, "Chipotle's Secret Salsa," *U.S. News & World Report,* January 9, 2008. Reprinted with permission.

Call it the "new pizza."

Just heat up a tortilla, pile on rice, beans, and whatever else you crave, wrap it up, and you're out the door.

As simple to make as its cheesy predecessor, the once humble burrito—previously the domain of mom and pop *taquería* joints in places like San Francisco's Mission District—has been reinvented and embraced by a new generation in which all things Latino aren't merely accepted as part of the American experience, they even have bling.

Just ask the folks lining up at Chipotle Mexican Grill, the most successful and perhaps the hippest of a collection of "fast casual" Mexican restaurants that together have swallowed up about 20 percent of the $11 billion quick-service restaurant market. Chipotle generates more than $1 billion in annual sales and has a stock market value of over $4 billion. Shares have more than quintupled in price since the company went public in 2006, though the stock has slipped some 20 percent since late last month as the overall market has tumbled on recession worries.

But the flood of burrito lovers hasn't abated. "Everybody who eats there just keeps going back, and they bring their friends," Dean Haskell, senior vice president of equity research at Morgan Joseph in Nashville, says of Chipotle's remarkable 12.4 percent sales growth at its restaurants open at least a year, more than double what Haskell had estimated for the third quarter. (Total sales were up 35.6 percent to $286 million.) "They have a great concept."

Chipotle is succeeding thanks to an elegantly simple business model, one its 42-year-old founder and CEO, Steve Ells, can sum up in a single sentence: "Focus on just a few things, and do them better than anybody else," he says of a menu that contains only three items: burritos, tacos, and salads. (The last was added only in 2005.)

Tough cookies. Of course, Chipotle's *taquería*-style format, in which 16 basic ingredients are displayed in front of customers on a glass-covered assembly line, affords a panoply of variations on its Mexican theme. Yet as anyone with a sweet tooth will quickly discover, there's not a sopaipilla, cup of flan, or even a cookie to be had in the joint. Restaurant analysts say that such additions at the end of the food line could instantly boost sales by 10 percent or more, something impressed upon Ells by executives at McDonald's, which until last year owned a majority stake in Chipotle.

Americans Think Fast Food Has Gotten Healthier

A 2009 survey of fast-food consumers showed that they think fast-food menus have gotten healthier in recent years. They have also not seen a dip in food quality at such restaurants.

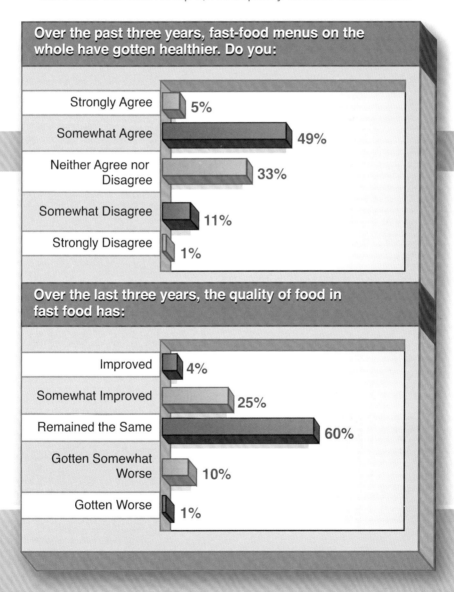

Over the past three years, fast-food menus on the whole have gotten healthier. Do you:

Strongly Agree	5%
Somewhat Agree	49%
Neither Agree nor Disagree	33%
Somewhat Disagree	11%
Strongly Disagree	1%

Over the last three years, the quality of food in fast food has:

Improved	4%
Somewhat Improved	25%
Remained the Same	60%
Gotten Somewhat Worse	10%
Gotten Worse	1%

Taken from: QSR Magazine, "What Consumers Say (Isn't Always What They Do)," June 2009.

But the company's single-minded founder has steadfastly rebuffed the idea. "We've had 10 years of double-digit comps in a row, and we've done that without cookies," he says. "So why start now? I see only the downside to adding cookies."

That's not to say that Ells refuses to tinker with a good thing. Trained at the prestigious Culinary Institute of America, Ells started his first Chipotle in 1993 near the University of Denver as a "cash cow" to help fund a "real restaurant." The shop was so busy that he quickly added four more eateries and then, with McDonald's financing, took the concept nationwide. Ells has continually upgraded Chipotle's basic ingredients and tweaked its recipes.

Take the time he called then company director Mats Lederhausen out of an important meeting. "He was screaming on the other end of the phone, 'I've found it! I've found it!'" the former McDonald's executive recalls of the eureka moment when Ells figured out what was wrong with the taste of Chipotle's black beans. "'They're not cutting the oregano in the right sizes!'"

"So?" Lederhausen said.

Ells then launched into a diatribe about "how the size of the oregano, when it mixes with the water, oil, and salt, doesn't embed the right taste layers in the beans," Lederhausen recalls. "Sure enough, the next time I tasted the beans, they were better."

Ells had a similar revelation seven years ago while trying to figure out why Chipotle's shredded-pork *carnitas* weren't selling as well as its grilled chicken or steak. On a trip to an Iowa hog farm that raised animals in the open, rather than in pens, he made a discovery: Because they put on more fat living out in the open, their meat was tastier.

Although the meat was more expensive, Chipotle soon switched to the free-range-pork supplier. "The ability to invest in higher-quality food as you increase sales is the thing that really drives the business," Ells says of a resulting doubling in *carnitas* sales.

Where's the pork? The idea has since been expanded into Chipotle's "Food with Integrity" initiative, which has adopted everything from humanely raised pork to hormone-free sour cream. Ells says that most of his customers don't know—and probably don't even care—whether the pork in their burrito is naturally raised, "but the higher-quality ingredients ultimately result in better-tasting food. No one else in the business can do that because their economic models are different."

To be sure, most purveyors of fast food, and even those in the more upscale "fast casual" category, have pursued a strategy of using the lowest-cost ingredients possible. In fact, "their labor costs are usually higher than their food costs," explains Chipotle Chief Operating Officer Monty Moran. "But for us, it's the other way around."

Chipotle founder Steve Ells shows off what makes Chipotle different from most fast food chains. Chipotle offers free-range meat.

While Chipotle pays competitive wages, starting at around $8.10 an hour, Ells and Moran have focused aggressively on serving customers quickly—increasing revenue per employee and pushing up average sales volumes to about $1.7 million per store annually. "That's pretty much unheard of in the industry," says Al Baldocchi, a restaurant consultant and longtime Chipotle director.

You can see the difference in Chipotle's kitchens, which despite requiring food preparation far more complex than the deep-fried, automated processes typical at most fast-food restaurants, are pictures of efficiency. "The grill area is right behind the chef's table, which is right behind the front line," Moran says of the streamlined setup. "So the people on the line just turn around when they need something, and it's ready."

Meanwhile, the company has taken full advantage of one of the economy's most important labor sources: Latinos, who now represent 80 percent of Chipotle's workforce. Eschewing part-timers and college students in favor of full-time, permanent employees, Moran has recently put a new, multitiered store management system in place that provides a path for line workers to move up. The result: one of the lowest employee turnover rates in the industry, "which is going to save a lot of money in the long run," notes analyst Haskell. "You get better people. And as they move up, their success just breeds more success."

So is Chipotle a "buy," after all?

"Well, let's just say this," Haskell says. "When they open up a store here in Nashville, I'll be first in line for a burrito

EVALUATING THE AUTHOR'S ARGUMENTS:

Markels says that restaurants like Chipotle are increasingly trying to show that fast food can be both fast and healthy. Do you think this is the wave of the future for fast food? In your opinion, will Americans start to demand that their fast food be made with higher quality, organic, or hormone-free products, even if it costs more? Why or why not?

Fast Food Makes People Fat

"America's favorite chains have . . . concocted thoroughly repellent dishes that make the Double Quarter Pounder look like a celery stick."

Brad Reed

In the following viewpoint Brad Reed describes seven fast-food dishes to argue that fast food makes people fat. He runs through dishes served at Starbucks, Kentucky Fried Chicken, Hardee's, and Domino's, some of which have more than a thousand calories and a hundred grams of fat per serving. In Reed's opinion, the creation of such foods is an assault on the American people, who already suffer from obesity in record high numbers. Reed thinks dishes like cheeseburger fries and Oreo pizza have no business being in existence because of the threat they pose to consumers' health.

Reed's articles have appeared in the *American Prospect* and Alternet.org, where this article was originally published. He also blogs at www.sadlyno.com.

AS YOU READ, CONSIDER THE FOLLOWING QUESTIONS:
1. How many calories does Reed say are in a single cheeseburger fry?
2. How many calories and grams of fat are in a Hardee's Monster Thickburger, according to Reed?
3. What is the KFC Double Down? What does the author find so offensive about it?

Brad Reed, "The Fast Food Industry's 7 Most Heinous Concoctions," AlterNet, August 27, 2009. www .alternet.org. Reproduced by permission.

Although the organic movement has certainly started to influence how Americans think about their food, it is still no match for the American fast food industry, which continuously finds creative new ways of piling sugar, salt and fat on a plate and charging customers $4.99 for the privilege of eating it.

In recent years, in fact, some of America's favorite chains have gone above and beyond the call of duty and concocted thoroughly repellent dishes that make the Double Quarter Pounder look like a celery stick. These companies have offered Americans these revolting meals despite the fact that roughly one-third of the country is now obese, a deplorable state of affairs that accounting firm Pricewaterhouse Coopers estimates costs the U.S. health-care system $200 billion a year in wasted spending.

In this article, we'll name and shame the very worst offenders, whether they're 1,400-calorie hamburgers or 550-calorie cups of coffee. So let's get things rolling with . . .

No. 7—The Krispy Kreme Doughnut Sundae
Two years ago, the brain trust at Krispy Kreme decided to answer the age-old question of how to make ice cream sundaes even less healthy. The solution, it turns out, is to remove bananas, strawberries or anything that looks remotely like it might contain nutrients, and replace it with a doughnut.

When the sundae—known affectionately as the Kool Kreme—premiered in Tacoma, [Washington], customers had the choice of adding several toppings, including bits of Snickers, Butterfinger, Heath and Junior Mints. They could add some fruit as well, of course, but what's the point? If you regularly eat a doughnut sundae, no level of Vitamin C will save you.

No. 6—Starbucks' Mocha Coconut Frappuccino Blended Coffee with Whipped Cream
At first glance, the Starbucks Mocha Coconut Frappuccino Blended Coffee with whipped cream doesn't seem to belong on this list. After all, its 550 calories and 22 grams of fat pale in comparison to some of the burgers and pizzas we'll encounter a little bit later. But then you remember that the Frappuccino is supposed to be a breakfast

drink. As in, something you drink the first thing in the morning while you eat your cereal. And then you understand that if you're willing to consume one-fourth of your daily caloric intake before you even arrive to work, there's nothing to stop you from wolfing down a 1,200-carlorie KFC [Kentucky Fried Chicken] Double Down (see Item No. 2) for lunch and dinner.

No. 5—Cheeseburger Fries

These treats were apparently made for people who love eating cheeseburgers and fries but who don't want to go through the hassle of mashing them together into a fine paste. Cheeseburger fries gained national attention when the *New York Times* reported that they had become a mini-sensation in the Midwest. The fries, said the *Times*, were "made of a meat-and-cheese compound" that was "breaded, then deep fried and served with ketchup or barbecue sauce." The caloric intake for these beasts was 75 calories per fry, meaning that eating 10 of them would account for more than a third of your daily intake.

> **FAST FACT**
>
> More than 9 million U.S. children and adolescents are obese. Almost one-third of youth eat at a fast-food restaurant on any given day, according to a 2009 study published in the *American Journal of Health*.

No. 4—The KFC Famous Bowl

KFC has a long and proud history of making Americans morbidly obese, but the company reached a new high in 2007 when it unleashed its Famous Bowl upon the world. The Bowl is really a variation on a classic American method of cooking that involves taking a bunch of unhealthy goo from different sources and then slopping them all into a bowl. In this particular example, KFC threw together mashed potatoes, corn, fried chicken, gravy and cheese to create a 720-calorie horror that contains 1 1/2 times your daily fat allowance. The thought of joylessly plowing through the Bowl's starchy potatoes, greasy gravy and processed cheese sounds about as soulless and monotonous as working in a puppy-slaughtering factory.

No. 3—Hardee's Monster Thickburger

Simply put, the Monster Thickburger is a fat, sloppy middle finger aimed at nutritionists everywhere. Clocking in at an artery-blowing 1,420 calories and 107 grams of fat, the Thickburger premiered in 2004, when McDonald's and Burger King were starting to sell out and offer their customers salads. In defending his decision to sell such a gaping monstrosity, Hardee's CEO [chief executive officer] Andrew Puzder played George W. Bush to McDonald's and Burger King's John Kerry, essentially calling them out as wimps who didn't have the balls to dramatically shorten their customers' life expectancy with just one meal. Specifically, he said the Thickburger was "not a burger for tree-huggers" but rather "for guys who want a really big, delicious, juicy decadent burger." Yes, gents, nothing will show the ladies how manly you are quite like a belly made entirely of butter.

No. 2—The KFC Double Down

Apparently determined to take the Atkins [high-calorie, low-carbohydrate] Diet to its most insane and illogical conclusion, KFC has released a new sandwich that succeeds in eliminating

Hardee's Monster Thickburger packs a walloping 1,420 calories and 107 grams of fat.

The Worst Fast-Food Cities in America

The following cities have the most fast-food restaurants per number of residents and also the highest percentage of people who visit them.

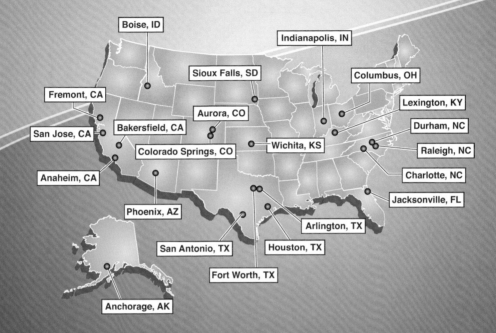

Boise, ID
Indianapolis, IN
Sioux Falls, SD
Columbus, OH
Fremont, CA
Lexington, KY
Aurora, CO
Durham, NC
San Jose, CA
Bakersfield, CA
Colorado Springs, CO
Wichita, KS
Raleigh, NC
Anaheim, CA
Charlotte, NC
Phoenix, AZ
Jacksonville, FL
Arlington, TX
San Antonio, TX
Houston, TX
Fort Worth, TX
Anchorage, AK

Taken from: Maria Masters, "Urban Waistlands," MSNBC, 2009. www.msnbc.com.

carbohydrate-packed bread by replacing it with two slabs of fried chicken. And oh yeah, in between the chicken they lay down heaping gobs of bacon and Swiss and pepper jack cheese. The KFC Double Down is really the ideological heir to the Thickburger, as it was seemingly designed for the sole purpose of pissing off nutrition advocates.

You can imagine future commercials where a rugged Ford-truck-style announcer comes on and says, "The next time some fruity bureaucrat tells you to exercise, look him in the eye and say, 'Hell no! I'm doublin' down with the KFC Double Down!'" The Double Down is slightly wimpier than the Thickburger as it only contains an estimated 1,200 calories. However, it more than makes up for this because it also contains something called "The Colonel's Sauce," which probably contains at the very least 2 percent all-natural radio-active waste.

No. 1—Domino's Oreo Cookie Pizza

Sure, everybody loves pizza. But what do you do when traditional pizza has lost its magic? How do you retain your love for it when all the fatty toppings—pepperoni, buffalo chicken, Alfredo sauce and so forth—just aren't satisfying you the way they used to? If you're Domino's, you take one of the world's least-healthy cookies and couple it with large doses of frosting to cover an entire pizza crust. Were Dr. Jack Kevorkian[1] still practicing his trade, he'd surely use consumption of the Oreo pizza as his preferred method of assisted suicide. Truly, the only way this sucker could be any worse would be to put it in a blender with a bucket of cheeseburger fries and then pour the resulting mixture into a bowl and then cover it with processed cheese. Which, come to think of it, hasn't been tried yet. Anyone want to drive me to the patent office?

EVALUATING THE AUTHORS' ARGUMENTS:

Brad Reed argues that fast-food companies have no business creating and offering some of the dishes they currently feature on their menus. How do you think J. Justin Wilson, author of the following viewpoint, would respond to this idea? With which author do you agree, and why?

1. An advocate for assisted suicide, Kevorkian became famous for helping elderly and sick people end their lives.

Viewpoint

4

Fast Food Does Not Make People Fat

J. Justin Wilson

"Census statistics indicate that none of the top 10 obese states have the most fast-food restaurants per person."

Fast food does not inherently make people fat, argues J. Justin Wilson in the following viewpoint. Rather, he claims, people make *themselves* fat when they overeat and get too little exercise. He points out that high rates of obesity do not correspond to numbers of fast-food restaurants—in fact, some states with low levels of obesity have high concentrations of fast-food restaurants, and some of the fattest states have the lowest concentrations of fast-food restaurants. Wilson says that fast food is not to blame for high rates of American obesity—but lack of exercise is. He urges people who are upset about obesity to put their energy toward programs that will encourage people to exercise and to leave fast-food companies alone.

Wilson is a senior research analyst at the Center for Consumer Freedom, a nonprofit coalition of restaurants, food companies, and consumers working together to promote personal responsibility.

AS YOU READ, CONSIDER THE FOLLOWING QUESTIONS:

1. Why, according to Wilson, is Colorado one of the leanest states despite having one of the highest concentrations of fast-food restaurants in the country?
2. How many "fat" states rank in the bottom fifteen for lowest concentration of fast-food restaurants?
3. What lesson does Wilson say is to be learned from Colorado?

Americans have access to the same food in every state. You will find the same soda in Tennessee as you will in Oregon. Fast-food franchises serve the same hamburgers in Arizona and in New Hampshire. Arkansas residents can buy the same packaged foods as residents of Ohio. Everyone, in every state, gets to decide what food to buy. Yet obesity rates vary widely across the country. With only a fifth of its residents officially fat, Colorado is the leanest state, while Mississippians, a third of whom are obese, are the fattest.

Obesity Is Not Related to Fast Food

These differences are puzzling to those convinced that obesity is simply the result of eating too much, or the wrong things. Do people in Mississippi really have the biggest appetites? State-by-state obesity trends make more sense when you look at the other side of the obesity equation: physical activity. Simply put, residents of states with high obesity rates tend to move less.

On a recent visit to Colorado, Kansas' *Wichita Eagle* food editor Joe Stumpe noticed that Colorado had all the usual fast-food eateries. So why is the state leaner than Kansas (which ranks 19th fattest in the nation)?

"[The] answer," Stumpe says, "does appear to involve walking,

FAST FACT

According to the Centers for Disease Control and Prevention, more than 50 percent of American adults do not get the recommended amount of physical activity necessary to provide health benefits. More than one-third of adolescents in grades nine to twelve do not exercise regularly.

running, skiing, boating, biking and a host of other physical activities. Colorado residents just seem to be more active than people in a lot of other states."

Lack of Exercise—Not Fast Food—Is the Problem

This observation was echoed by co-founder of the National Weight Control Registry, James Hill. He suggests that people's failure to get trimmer can be attributed in large part to our narrow, food-only approach. "We focus too much on diet and not enough on physical activity," he says.

Both Stumpe and Hill's hunches are backed by the facts. Of the top 10 most-obese states, government surveys show nine of them are also the most sedentary. The residents of the most obese state—Mississippi—report the lowest rates of leisure-time physical activity in the country.

Some experts contend that lack of exercise, rather than fast food, is the cause of obesity in the United States.

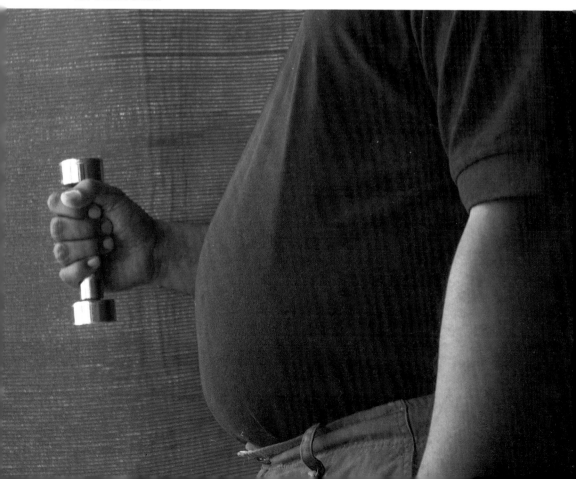

No Correlation Between Obesity and Number of Restaurants

Are fast-food outlets too numerous? Census statistics indicate that none of the top 10 obese states have the most fast-food restaurants per person. And seven out of those ten "fat" states rank in the 15 lowest concentration of fast food. In fact, the heaviest state—

Americans Do Not Think Fast-Food Restaurants Are Responsible for Their Health

A national Gallup Poll found that the majority of Americans believe it is an individual's responsibility to avoid obesity by making healthy choices when eating. Most Americans do not lay the blame for the nation's obesity problem at the door of fast-food restaurants.

"How responsible is the fast-food industry for the health problems faced by obese people in this country: very responsible, somewhat responsible, not too responsible, or not responsible at all?"

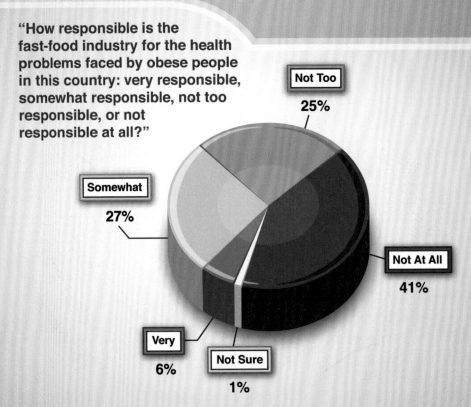

Not Too
25%

Somewhat
27%

Not At All
41%

Very
6%

Not Sure
1%

Taken from: Gallup Poll, July 7–9, 2003.

Mississippi—is third lowest in the country. Colorado—the leanest state—is among the ten states that have the highest concentration of fast-food restaurants.

This reality is mirrored by scholarly studies. A 2007 study published in the *International Journal of Obesity* concludes, "The obesity epidemic is often speculatively blamed on fast food, when the actual evidence shows very little, if any, association of fast food with weight gain." There is an unambiguous relationship between physical inactivity and obesity in the United States. At the same time, there is no clear relationship between obesity and access to fast-food restaurants.

Reduce Obesity with Exercise, Not with Fast-Food Laws

The self-appointed food police in society don't like those facts. Because controlling food prices or availability is easier than controlling people's physical activity, these activists push for new laws that range from warning labels to new taxes on anything caloric.

The ultimate goal of food activists is the prohibition of high-calorie foods. As one activist put it, "there is no difference between Ronald McDonald and Joe Camel." Statistics tell us that the nutritional content of our meals is virtually unchanged from a half-century ago, but fewer of us are burning off the calories we ingest. If there's a lesson to learn from Colorado, it's this: Have a soft drink with lunch, or a beer with your dinner—but don't forget to go for a walk. If they can do it in Denver, so can you.

> **EVALUATING THE AUTHORS' ARGUMENTS:**
>
> J. Justin Wilson argues that fast food is not the main reason people get fat. How do you think the other authors in this chapter would respond to this claim? Write two or three sentences per author on what you think they would say. Then, state your own opinion on the matter. Does fast food make people fat, or do people make themselves fat when they fail to take care of themselves?

Fast-Food Restaurants Are Responsible for Causing Disease

Susan J. Douglas

In the following viewpoint Susan J. Douglas accuses fast-food restaurants of contributing to high rates of disease in Americans. She says that fast-food companies offer high-fat, high-calorie foods that are known to cause diabetes, which is a leading cause of blindness and kidney failure and can even result in amputation and death. But far from innocently making their products available to any American who wants them, Douglas says fast-food chains target low-income people of color because they are less likely to be able to afford higher-quality food. Also, many of these people are immigrants who associate fast food with typical American culture. Douglas concludes it is reasonable for Americans to sue fast-food companies for endangering their health because those companies are responsible for making Americans sick.

"The fast food gauntlet on the main streets in Flushing [Queens] . . . pulls in recent Asian immigrants who pick up diabetes along with the burger and fries."

Susan J. Douglas, "Let Them Eat Crap," *In These Times,* January 24, 2006. Reproduced by permission of the publisher. www.inthesetimes.com.

Douglas is a professor of communications at the University of Michigan.

AS YOU READ, CONSIDER THE FOLLOWING QUESTIONS:
1. What is the "illness-industrial complex," as described by Douglas?
2. According to Douglas, what is the rate of diabetes in the wealthy Upper East Side of New York? What is the rate of diabetes in poorer Spanish Harlem?
3. How much does Douglas say the food industry spends each year marketing its products to kids?

"Begin on the sixth floor, third room from the end, swathed in fluorescence: a 60-year-old woman was having two toes sawed off." So opened the *New York Times'* four-part series in early January [2006], "Bad Blood," about the Type 2 diabetes epidemic in New York City. Type 2 diabetes is caused by excess weight, lack of exercise and poor diet, and is directly related to poverty.

The series reminded one that poverty has a map. Indeed, even if you did not read every word of "Bad Blood"—each story started on the front page and took up two full pages inside—eye-catching illustrations showed the dividing line between poverty and wealth (96th Street on the Upper East Side) and the fast food gauntlet on the main streets in Flushing [Queens], which pulls in recent Asian immigrants who pick up diabetes along with the burger and fries.

The Illness-Industrial Complex

Diabetes is the leading cause of blindness and kidney failure in the country; it often leads to amputation. It's the sixth leading cause of death in the United States and costs us $132 billion a year. And it's preventable, save for the enormous financial interests involved in its preservation. "Bad Blood" brought together three American scandals—poverty, our morally bankrupt for-profit health care system and the practices of our nation's fast food joints.

Combined, they make up an illness-industrial complex, in which big players in the food industry, insurance industry and medical establishment profit wildly. But they need more raw materials to keep them going, more fodder for their assembly lines. Poor people of color are that fodder, and very few of the rest of America seems to care.

Fast Food Chains Target Poor People of Color

Remember the summer of 2002 when a lawyer filed suit against McDonald's and other fast food restaurants? His two teenage clients, one 5-foot-6 and 270 pounds, the other 4-feet-10 and 140 pounds, routinely ate fast food and were diabetic. He charged that McDonald's did not provide easy-to-understand nutritional information about its fast food, nor disclose that additives made its food less healthy than represented in its ads. The suit immediately became a laughingstock: how preposterous to hold McDonald's accountable for your own overeating! The National Restaurant Association, however, was far from amused.

FAST FACT

The risk of stroke increases by 13 percent for those living in close proximity to fast-food restaurants, according to a February 2009 study presented at the International Stroke Conference in San Diego.

The *Times'* main point is that Type 2 diabetes is an epidemic that promises to grow widely. But its consequences are seriously underappreciated because the disease's victims are disproportionately poor people of color. The Centers for Disease Control and Prevention project that one in three children—one in three!— born five years ago will become diabetic sometime in their lives. But this will be unequally distributed. The *Times* showed that below 96th Street on the Upper East Side, with a median income of $75,000 and a poverty rate of 6.2 percent, only 1 percent of the population has diabetes. Up in Spanish Harlem, where the median income is $20,000 and the poverty rate 38.2 percent, 16 percent have diabetes.

The Fast Food Conspiracy That Is Making People Sick

There's just something about this that seems, well, like a business plan. Budget cuts have simultaneously forced schools to eliminate P.E. classes

In Spanish Harlem in New York, over half the population is obese or overweight, conditions that can cause diabetes. Some experts believe that the food on menus at McDonald's and other fast-food restaurants is making people ill.

and make up for lost revenue by installing Coke and candy machines in the halls. The food industry spends $10 billion a year marketing foods to kids, and we're not talking carrots and celery. Clustered in poor neighborhoods, fast food joints continue to hawk 64 oz. sodas and items like Burger King's Enormous Omelet Sandwich (730 calories, 47 grams of fat). Once poor folk are fattened for the kill, the insurance companies step in. According to the *Times*, health care providers make a profit when they amputate a limb or provide a prosthetic, but lose money if they seek to prevent blindness or provide nutritional advice.

Because this sickening cycle is *only* the result of individual (not industrial) greed, in October [2006] the House of Representatives passed, by a 306–120 vote, the "Personal Responsibility in Food Consumption Act" (a.k.a., the "cheeseburger bill"), which would protect the food industry from obesity-related lawsuits. Kentucky Republican Mitch McConnell's companion "Commonsense

Consumption Act," awaits action in the Senate. Already 20 states have enacted their own versions of "commonsense consumption" laws. Guess who wrote them? Lobbyists for the food industry.

Fast-Food Chains Cannot Get Away with Making People Sick

According to Melanie Warner, writing in the *Times'* business pages, the National Restaurant Association, with headquarters in

Washington and 50 state organizations, has led the individual responsibility campaign, dispatching restaurant owners and food executives to the statehouses and Congress. In the last two congressional elections, the food and restaurant industry gave a total of $5.5 million to politicians in the 20 states that have passed laws shielding companies from obesity liability.

The illness-industrial complex is betting that they will get away with this. That's what the tobacco companies thought too.

Fast-Food Restaurants Are Not Responsible for Causing Disease

Jacob Sullum

> *"It's possible that people who eat a lot of fried chicken don't worry about the nutritional profile of their food."*

In the following viewpoint Jacob Sullum argues that fast-food restaurants are not to blame for diseases such as obesity in Americans. Sullum says that people who have tried to sue fast-food companies for making them sick have no ground to stand on: First, fast-food companies publicly post the ingredients in their food, so no consumer has an excuse for not knowing what they are eating; second, it is up to consumers to make decisions about the food they put in their bodies. Most people know that fast food is not the healthiest choice but eat it anyway because they like the taste. Sullum also says this is why people ignore the fact that fast food contains trans fats—an unhealthy kind of fat that has been linked to heart disease, liver dysfunction,

Jacob Sullum, "The Fried Logic of Food Police," Reason.com, August 18, 2006. http://reason.com. Reproduced by permission of Reason Foundation.

and Alzheimer's disease. For all these reasons, Sullum says fast-food restaurants are not to blame if Americans want to eat their products knowing full well what they contain.

Sullum is a nationally syndicated columnist and a senior editor at *Reason* magazine, in which this viewpoint was originally published.

AS YOU READ, CONSIDER THE FOLLOWING QUESTIONS:
1. Who is Arthur Hoyte, and how does he factor into the author's argument?
2. Why, according to Sullum, do fast-food restaurants use partially hydrogenated vegetable oil in their foods?
3. What two lawsuits have been threatened by the Center for Science in the Public Interest, according to Sullum?

Remember Caesar Barber, the New York maintenance worker who blamed McDonald's for making him fat? "They said, '100 percent beef.' I thought that meant it was good for you," he claimed in July 2002.

Barber's story was harder to swallow than a super-sized Big Mac meal. So what are we to make of Arthur Hoyte, a retired physician from Rockville, Maryland, who is suing KFC [Kentucky Fried Chicken] because he thought fried chicken was a health food? In a lawsuit sponsored by the Center for Science in the Public Interest [CSPI], Hoyte claims he had no idea the restaurant chain fries its food in partially hydrogenated vegetable oil. "If I had known that KFC uses an unnatural frying oil, and that the food was so high in trans fat, I would have reconsidered my choices," he says.

Aren't doctors supposed to be smart, at least when it comes to health-related issues? If Hoyte has no way of knowing about all the trans fat in KFC's dishes, what chance do the rest of us have?

Fast-Food Restaurants Make Ingredients Public Knowledge

CSPI's would-be class action, based on Washington, D.C. consumer protection law, accuses the chain of failing to disclose "material facts" about its food and demands that it either stop using partially

Kentucky Fried Chicken has been accused of failing to disclose that it uses unhealthy, partially-hydrogenated cooking oil to fry its chicken.

hydrogenated oil or post trans fat warning signs. According to CSPI Executive Director Michael Jacobson (who is not known for his rhetorical subtlety), KFC "recklessly puts its customers at risk of a Kentucky Fried Coronary" and is "making its unsuspecting consumers' arteries Extra Crispy." To support these claims, CSPI's online statement links to three pages of nutritional information about the KFC menu.

But who is that bearded, white-haired gentleman in the upper left corner of each page in this damning indictment? It turns out the trans fat secrets Colonel Sanders is keeping from his customers—information so arcane even a medical specialist cannot reasonably be expected to know it—is contained in a "Nutrition Guide" on KFC's Web site and on big, conspicuous posters in KFC outlets.

People Do Not Really Care What Is in Fast Food

The use of partially hydrogenated vegetable oil by restaurants is widely known; they switched to it after groups like CSPI complained about the animal fat and tropical oils they had been using. At the time, the new fat was thought to be healthier, but subsequent research has indicated it may in fact be worse. A man of medicine like Dr. Hoyte surely was aware of this development.

The problem, from CSPI's point of view, is not that people don't know about trans fat in KFC's food but that they don't care. If there were a big enough demand for trans-fat-free fried chicken, KFC would make the switch to nonhydrogenated vegetable oil (which costs more and has a shorter shelf life). But it's possible that people who eat a lot of fried chicken don't worry about the nutritional profile of their food.

A Proper Diet Cannot Be Enforced

As usual, CSPI does not like the choices consumers are making and wants businesses to follow its preferences instead. The organization brags about using the threat of a lawsuit to pressure the leading soda manufacturers into an agreement aimed at removing sugar-sweetened beverages from public schools—a deal that is not likely to have a noticeable impact on students' waistlines but may inspire restrictions on adults, such as "junk-food-free" zones near schools. In Massachusetts, CSPI is threatening to sue Kellogg, maker of sugary breakfast cereals, and Viacom, owner of TV channels and cartoon characters used to market "nutritionally poor" food. CSPI argues that children are injured every time they see an ad for Apple Jacks or a box of SpongeBob SquarePants Pop-Tarts, whether or not their parents actually buy the product.

> **FAST FACT**
>
> McDonald's offers a menu with eight meal choices for people with diabetes. Each menu item lists calories, carbohydrates, and fat content so that those with diabetes can monitor their sugar intake.

Americans Do Not Care Whether Fast Food Is Healthy

A 2009 poll of fast-food customers found that the vast majority agreed that Subway offers the healthiest fast food. Yet only 10 percent of respondents say they visit Subway regularly. Polls like this suggest that Americans are more interested in how their food tastes than in how healthy it is.

Which chain offers the healthiest menu choices?

Chain	Percent
Subway	54%
Panera Bread	8%
Wendy's	8%
Boston Market	6%
Quiznos	5%
McDonald's	3%
Arby's	3%
Blimpie	2%
Chick-fil-A	2%
KFC	2%
Starbucks	2%

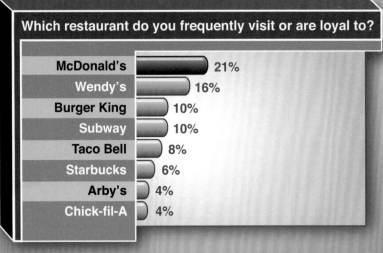

Which restaurant do you frequently visit or are loyal to?

Restaurant	Percent
McDonald's	21%
Wendy's	16%
Burger King	10%
Subway	10%
Taco Bell	8%
Starbucks	6%
Arby's	4%
Chick-fil-A	4%

Taken from: *QSR Magazine*, "What Consumers Say (Isn't Always What They Do)," June 2009.

Each of these cases supposedly is about damage suffered and compensation owed. But the real goal is to impose CSPI's ideas about a proper diet on consumers who have different values and priorities. If this is in "the public interest," it's an interest the public itself is too benighted [unenlightened] to recognize.

> **EVALUATING THE AUTHOR'S ARGUMENTS:**
>
> Jacob Sullum's argument hinges on the assumption that Americans know fast food is bad for them—but they eat it because they do not care. Do you think this is a fair assumption to make? Why or why not? Use evidence from the texts you have read to form your answer.

Chapter 2

Should Fast Food Be Regulated?

America's propensity for wolfing down fast food has caused some to argue that the industry should be strictly regulated; others claim to do so would infringe on Americans' right to eat what they like.

Fast-Food Restaurants Should Be Banned in Certain Areas

"Banning fast food around schools will have a measurable impact on students' lives, and will help them grow up to be healthier, stronger adults."

Peter Milosheff

In the following viewpoint Peter Milosheff explains why fast-food restaurants should be banned near schools. He draws on a study conducted by the University of California and Columbia University that showed students who go to school within 0.1 miles of a fast-food restaurant are more likely to be obese. Because fast food tastes good to kids, and because it tends to be advertised in connection with fun toys and popular movie characters, Milosheff asserts that placing fast-food restaurants near schools is unfair; children are too vulnerable to be highly exposed to them. Milosheff and others believe that banning fast-food restaurants near schools can reduce childhood obesity and later cases of cancer, diabetes, high blood pressure, and other health problems.

Peter Milosheff, "Ban Fast Food <0.1 Miles of Schools," *Bronx Times,* May 5, 2009. www.bronx.com. Reproduced by permission.

Milosheff is the president and chief executive officer of the *Bronx Times* and Bronx.com, where this viewpoint was originally published.

AS YOU READ, CONSIDER THE FOLLOWING QUESTIONS:
1. By what percent does obesity increase when a school is 0.1 miles from a fast-food restaurant, as reported by Milosheff?
2. What does the word "predatory" mean in the context of the viewpoint?
3. How many schools are within 0.1 miles of a fast-food restaurant in the Manhattan–East Harlem neighborhood, according to the author?

Today [May 5, 2009], following the release of a study showing that students whose schools are within 0.1 miles of fast food outlets are more likely to be obese, and with diabetes a growing epidemic in New York City, Councilman Eric Gioia (D-Queens) and MeMe Roth, President of National Action Against Obesity (NAAO), announced Gioia will introduce legislation to ban fast food stores within 0.1 miles of schools.

The study, conducted by the University of California [at Berkeley] and Columbia University [New York City], examined millions of school children across the country. A preliminary investigation by Gioia found that neighborhoods with the highest obesity rates across the City had 28 fast food restaurants within 0.1 miles of schools.

Fast Food Restaurants Poison Students

Several national state, and City organizations, including NAAO, the Hunger Action Network of NY State, the Healthy Schools Network, and the New York Coalition for Healthy School Food, have expressed support for Gioia's proposal.

"Children are literally being poisoned by their food environments," said Councilman Gioia. "This study has confirmed what many of us have known for years: that proximity to fast food leads to an unhealthy lifestyle. Banning fast food around schools will have a measurable impact on students' lives, and will help them grow up to be healthier, stronger adults."

"Our results clearly show that children whose schools are located very close to fast food outlets (within 0.1 miles) are more likely to be overweight. This does not seem to be because of other characteristics of these children and neighborhoods. Hence, legislation that restricted access to fast food by school age children might help the epidemic of childhood obesity," said Janet Currie, a co-author of the report, and the Sami Mnaymneh Professor of Economics and Chair [of the] Department of Economics at Columbia University.

Kids Prefer French Fries and Pizza to Juice and Sandwiches

Kids love french fries and order them more often than other fast-food selections, according to a marketing company that studies fast-food trends.

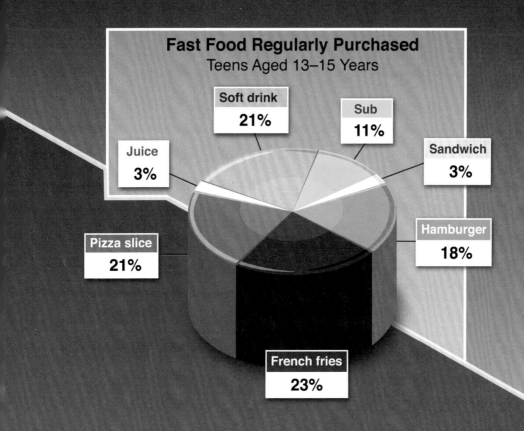

Fast Food Regularly Purchased
Teens Aged 13–15 Years

Soft drink 21%

Sub 11%

Juice 3%

Sandwich 3%

Pizza slice 21%

Hamburger 18%

French fries 23%

Taken from: Speed Fry Corporation, 2006.

Banning Fast Food Near Schools Keeps Students Safe

"NAAO—and I personally as a parent to two New York City public school students—ardently support the proposal to keep junk food establishments at least 0.1 miles from New York City's schools. NAAO believes predatory marketing of junk food escalates the child obesity health crisis. Research reveals that fast food restaurants' close proximity to schools increases child obesity. It's time to applaud and enact Councilman Gioia's proposals to create School Safety Zones for New York City's children," said MeMe Roth, President of the National Action Against Obesity.

> **FAST FACT**
>
> In 2009 researchers from the University of California at Berkeley and Columbia University reported that teens who go to school within one-tenth of a mile of a fast-food restaurant are more likely to be obese than their peers. In fact, the incidence of obesity increased 5.2 percent in schools that were located 530 feet or less from a fast-food outlet.

"Obesity is a significant and growing problem among New York's children, including those that are low-income. We applaud Councilman Gioia's continued leadership to improve nutrition in our communities," said Mark Dunlea, Executive Director of the Hunger Action Network of New York State. "Increased government action restricting children's access to unhealthy foods is long overdue. In addition, we hope that state lawmakers finally pass the Healthy Schools Act to end the sale of junk food in our schools and to strengthen nutritional standards for school meals."

When Fast Food Is Near Schools, Kids Suffer

The University of California and Columbia report, titled *The Effect of Fast Food Restaurants On Obesity*, found a clear link between obesity in 9th graders and the distance of fast food from schools. The report found:

- [A] 5.2 % increase in the incidence of obesity when a school is 0.1 miles from a fast food restaurant.

- The proximity of fast food can increase caloric intake of 30 to 100 calories per school-day.
- The effect is largest for Hispanic students and female students.
- When fast food is 0.25 or 0.5 miles from a school there is no effect on obesity rates.
- The presence of non–fast food restaurants is not related to obesity and weight gain.
- Restricting access to fast food near schools could have effects on obesity among children.

In order to help stem the epidemic of childhood obesity and diabetes, and to promote a healthier lifestyle for New York's school children, Gioia announced he will introduce legislation which would ban fast food restaurants from locating within 0.1 miles of a school. Current fast food restaurants would be exempted from the ban, but after the legislation is enacted, fast food would be forbidden from moving into that location.

Preying on Children

"Fast food restaurants locating next to schools is a predatory practice. This cheap, low quality food has both short and long term health consequences," said Amie Hamlin, Executive Director of New York Coalition for Healthy School Food. "In our society, healthy food is not the convenient choice nor the least expensive choice, and this needs to change. We have found students actually enjoy good tasting healthy food."

A preliminary investigation of neighborhoods in each borough with the highest obesity rates found many fast food restaurants within 0.1 miles of schools. The investigation found:

- Staten Island [SI]—Northern SI (31.3% obesity rate): 2 schools within 0.1 miles of a fast food restaurant.
- Bronx—South Bronx (34% obesity rate): 8 schools within 0.1 miles of 1 fast food restaurant, and 1 school within 0.1 miles of 2 fast food restaurants.
- Brooklyn—Bedford-Stuyvesant: (31.3% obesity rate): 2 schools within 0.1 miles of a fast food restaurant.
- Manhattan—East Harlem (31.7% obesity rate): 18 schools within 0.1 miles of a total of 17 different fast food restaurants.

A student in Harlem walks past one of the twelve fast-food restaurants located within a block of his school.

A total of 12 schools in East Harlem had multiple fast food restaurants within a block walking distance. James Weldon Johnson Elementary School had a total of 5 fast food restaurants within a block.

Statistics show that obesity is an increasing problem throughout New York City:

- 40% of children in Harlem are obese.
- Nearly half of all New York City elementary schoolchildren are not at a healthy weight.
- In New York City, 1 in 5 kindergarten children is obese. The rate of childhood obesity in the City is over twice the national average.
- Data shows that obesity begins early in life: nearly half of all elementary school children and Head Start children [those enrolled in a federally funded preschool program for low-income families] are not a healthy weight. In fact, 1 in 4 children in Head Start programs are obese.

Fast Food Is Too Dangerous Not to Regulate

Other municipalities have taken steps to combat obesity by restricting fast food. In July of 2008, Los Angeles passed legislation which banned free-standing fast food restaurants from the West Adams, Baldwin Hills, and Leimert Community plan areas, along with South Los Angeles and Southeast Los Angeles. Los Angeles found that 45% of the 900 restaurants in the poor neighborhoods of South Los Angeles were fast food, as compared with only 16% of the 2,200 restaurants in West Los Angeles.

"Healthy Schools Network supports Councilman Gioia's effort to reduce the exposure of vulnerable children to unhealthy 'fast food' outlets near schools. Healthy children learn better, stay healthy and can grow to become healthy adults. We support wholesome foods for healthy development and learning," said Claire Barnett, Executive Director, Healthy Schools Network, Inc.

Fast food is extremely unhealthy and can lead to a variety of health problems—and has been directly linked to obesity. According to the *Lancet* medical journal, those who frequently eat fast food gained 10 pounds more than those who did less often. Those who eat fast food with regularity were more than twice as likely to develop diabetes. In 2003, a study found that nearly 1 in 3 children ages 4 to 19 ate fast food every day, and that fast food adds approximately 6 extra pounds per year. That same study found that fast food consumption by children had increased fivefold since 1970. There are several health consequences of obesity, including heart disease, diabetes, cancer, hypertension (high blood pressure), liver and gallbladder disease, and sleep apnea and respiratory problems.

EVALUATING THE AUTHOR'S ARGUMENTS:

Peter Milosheff reports on some of the consequences of fast-food restaurants being near schools. Think about where your school is located. Are any fast-food restaurants on campus or just off campus? Which ones? Do you think their presence is dangerous? Why or why not?

Fast-Food Restaurants Should Not Be Banned Anywhere

Sara Wexler

"Banning fast-food restaurants will not solve the obesity problem, nor will any other laws that scapegoat the food industry and ignore personal responsibility."

Fast-food restaurants should never be banned, argues Sara Wexler in the following viewpoint. She discusses an effort in Los Angeles to ban fast-food restaurants in low-income neighborhoods that have high rates of obesity. But Wexler says such a ban is insulting to residents in the area because it implies they have no self-control or personal responsibility for what they eat. Additionally, there are no guarantees that healthy, affordable restaurants will take the place of fast-food restaurants. Ultimately, Wexler thinks fast-food restaurant bans fail to address the root causes of obesity, which have more to do with general disinterest in being healthy than with the availability of fast food. For this reason, she thinks restaurant bans are a misguided response to the problem of obesity in America.

Sara Wexler, "Fat Chance," *The American,* August 21, 2008. Reproduced with the permission of the American Enterprise Institute for Public Policy Research, Washington, D.C.

Wexler is a research assistant at the American Enterprise Institute, a public policy organization that supports limited government and private enterprise.

AS YOU READ, CONSIDER THE FOLLOWING QUESTIONS:
1. In what way does Wexler say a fast-food restaurant ban might raise food prices in neighborhoods? In what way might it lower them?
2. What did a menu analysis of twenty-four national chains find about sit-down restaurants as compared to fast-food restaurants?
3. In Wexler's opinion, why is exempting restaurants like Marie Callender's or Subway from a fast-food ban not fair?

At a time when public officials across America are finding creative ways to combat the "obesity epidemic," the Los Angeles City Council has decided to try a radical approach: it is seeking to regulate the number of fast-food restaurants in the mainly low-income neighborhoods of south Los Angeles through zoning controls. Permits for fast-food restaurants will not be issued in a 32-square-mile section of the city. Though the ban is only effective for one year, it is renewable for two six-month increments—and its sponsors are hoping to make it permanent. Other cities, New York in particular, are considering whether to adopt similar regulations.

Banning Fast Food Is Insulting to Customers and Companies

The fast-food ban has been promoted as an economic development plan designed to bring more dining options to the community, such as sit-down restaurants and supermarkets. Its supporters cite the high obesity rates in south Los Angeles. (Approximately 30 percent of south L.A. residents are obese, in comparison to 21 percent in the rest of L.A. County and 25.6 percent nationwide.) They believe the fast-food ban will help reduce obesity and also save taxpayer money, since obesity places enormous costs on the California state Medicare system.

However, critics compare it to a mandate that everyone eat salads and lose weight. Hans Bader of the Competitive Enterprise Institute

Los Angeles councilwoman Jan Perry has drawn criticism for legislation banning new fast-food restaurants in the poor neighborhoods of south Los Angeles.

and William Saletan of Slate have examined the racial and socioeconomic implications. As Bader points out, many civil rights groups that support the fast-food ban were outraged when a Domino's Pizza franchise refused to deliver to certain neighborhoods. Saletan criticizes the City Council for "depicting poor people . . . as less capable of free choice." Others complain that the ban defies economics. Both fast-food and sit-down restaurants are being asked to ignore their own economic interests. As the California Restaurant Association notes, if the south L.A. market demanded sit-down restaurants, they would already be there.

The Unintended Consequences of a Ban

The fast-food ban may have unintended consequences. Without the threat of incoming competition, existing fast-food restaurants in south L.A. can feel free to raise their prices; fast-food restaurants have already done this in cities with high barriers to entry, such as New York. Additionally, an influx of sit-down restaurants could increase the average price of a meal

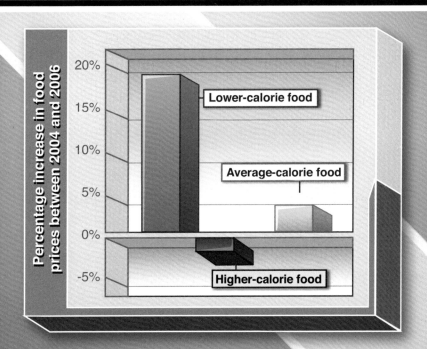

Healthy Food Is Expensive

The price of healthy fresh food rose dramatically between 2004 and 2006. However, the cost of high-calorie food, like fast food, dropped. Some say fast food should not be banned because it is an affordable option in low-income neighborhoods.

Percentage increase in food prices between 2004 and 2006

Lower-calorie food

Average-calorie food

Higher-calorie food

Taken from: *Los Angeles Times*, "The Price of Healthful Food."

in south L.A., since sit-down establishments are generally more costly than fast-food outlets. On the other hand, fast-food prices might also go *down* in response to the arrival of costlier sit-down restaurants, thus encouraging residents to forego the sit-down restaurant and eat more of the cheaper fast food. Indeed, there is no guarantee that additional supermarkets and fresh-food restaurants will cause south L.A. residents to abandon fast food.

Fast Food Is Not the Only Culprit

The ban implies that fast food is a major cause of obesity; yet the food served at sit-down restaurants, particularly the chain restaurants most likely to enter south L.A., often has significantly higher calorie and fat counts than the food served at restaurants like McDonald's, Burger King, and Wendy's. According to David Zinczenko, editor-in-chief of *Men's Health* magazine, the average meal at a sit-down chain restaurant is generally *less* healthy than a comparable fast-food meal. As Zinczenko writes, the food at a sit-down chain "is actually considerably worse for you than the often-maligned fast-food fare. In fact, our menu analysis of 24 national chains revealed that the average entree at a sit-down restaurant contains 867 calories, compared with 522 calories in the average fast-food entree. And that's before appetizers, sides, or desserts—selections that can easily double your total calorie intake."

> ## FAST FACT
>
> In 2008 the Los Angeles City Council passed a city ordinance that bans the construction of new fast-food restaurants in a thirty-two-square-mile area where 500,000 low-income people live.

Because the definition of "fast food" is somewhat vague, restaurants like Marie Callender's (which specializes in pies and hearty fare) can still open, yet mom-and-pop take-out restaurants and other local establishments can still be banned. Exceptions have also been carved out for "healthy" fast-food restaurants like Subway, which does have its six subs under six grams of fat but also serves several 12-inch sandwiches with more than 1,000 calories.

Fast-Food Ban Does Not Address the Real Causes of Obesity

The major problem with the fast-food ban is that it doesn't address the real causes of obesity: a lack of personal responsibility and a lack of motivation to stay healthy. Unfortunately, a recent wave of obesity lawsuits has targeted the fast-food industry and ignored any concept of personal responsibility. To their credit, some U.S. lawmakers have tried to prevent such litigation. The "Cheeseburger Bill" (the Personal Responsibility in Food Consumption Act) was designed to protect restaurants from obesity lawsuits. It passed the House of Representatives but died in the Senate in 2005. The [George W.] Bush administration has supported the federal Cheeseburger Bill and also backed similar legislation at the state level, arguing that "food manufacturers and sellers should not be held liable for injury because of a person's consumption of legal, unadulterated food and a person's weight gain or obesity." California has not passed any such legislation, leaving fast-food restaurants in the Golden State vulnerable to obesity lawsuits.

If the L.A. City Council wants to encourage healthier eating in low-income communities, incentives and disincentives would be a more reasonable and effective path. Fried foods could be taxed, or fast food in general could be taxed (though this tax would be just as regressive as the ban). But banning fast-food restaurants will not solve the obesity problem, nor will any other laws that scapegoat the food industry and ignore personal responsibility.

> **EVALUATING THE AUTHOR'S ARGUMENTS:**
>
> One of the points Sara Wexler raises in her argument is that banning fast-food restaurants is unfair to the fast-food companies that have a right to sell their food. What do you think—does a company always have a right to sell its product? Why or why not? Can you think of some companies that do not always have the right to sell their product? Offer at least three examples.

Fast Food Should Be Taxed

Martin B. Schmidt

"If the low 'cost' of eating fast food is adding to the obesity problem, the solution involves increasing the cost, even in a nominal way."

Taxing fast food can have several benefits, suggests Martin B. Schmidt in the following viewpoint. He argues that fast food has become a big problem: It contributes to obesity and has also become so inexpensive and convenient that it is almost impossible for Americans to avoid. Therefore, Schmidt suggests imposing a tax on drive-through fast-food purchases. Such a tax would have several purposes, he says. First, it might get people out of their cars and make them walk into the restaurant to avoid the tax. Second, the money generated from the tax could go toward helping to pay for the outrageous costs of obesity. Finally, paying a tax on their fast food might cause some people to stop and consider carefully the food choices they make. For all of these reasons, Schmidt thinks fast food should be taxed.

Schmidt is an economics professor at the College of William and Mary in Williamsburg, Virginia.

The National Center for Health Statistics estimates that 30 percent of American adults, some 60 million people, are obese. Thirty years ago that number was 15 percent. The trend is similar among children: according to the surgeon general, the percentage of obese youths has tripled, to nearly 15 percent, since the 1960's.

Obviously, we face a crisis of obesity and its concomitant health problems. In the spirit of "every little thing can help," I have a modest suggestion to reverse the trend: enact a tax on drive-through food orders.

Food Has Become "Too Cheap"

Now there are many reasons for the rise in obesity, but to an economist a big factor is that food has become "too cheap." I do not mean in the typical sense of dollars and cents. (The fact that that the average family pays only about 20 percent of its income on food today, down from 30 percent in the 1960's, is a positive change.)

Rather, I mean that the procurement of food has become too "cheap" in terms of time and effort. Advances in technology have allowed us to increase the food supply while reducing the amount of workers needed to produce it. In 1830, roughly 300 labor-hours were required to produce 100 bushels of wheat. Today, that number of bushels can be produced with fewer than three labor-hours.

FAST FACT

A July 2009 Kaiser Family Foundation survey found that 55 percent of respondents said they "strongly favor" or "somewhat favor" an increase in tax on unhealthy foods.

At the same time, of course, workers have moved into less physically taxing jobs, typically spending most of the day sitting in a chair rather than tilling the soil. Some estimates hold that 50 percent of Americans do no exercise regularly.

Americans Need Incentives to Change Their Ways

And in terms of breakfast, lunch and dinner, one hardly has to do anything but drive a car and chew. The Centers for Disease Control and Prevention estimates that 40 percent of the average family's food budget is spent on fast food. Furthermore, a recent study from the market survey firm Claritas estimates that 78 percent of all fast-food diners use the drive-through. Heck, even many of the more expensive, family-style restaurant chains now have special parking spaces where video cameras are on the lookout so workers can bring your order to you in the front seat.

Proponents of a drive-through food tax say it will motivate Americans to get out of their cars and walk into restaurants.

Tax Junk Food to Pay for Health Care

A 2009 poll revealed that the majority of Americans favor taxing junk food. The proceeds from these taxes could be used to cover the high costs of obesity and health care.

Would you favor or oppose each of the following to help pay for health care reform:

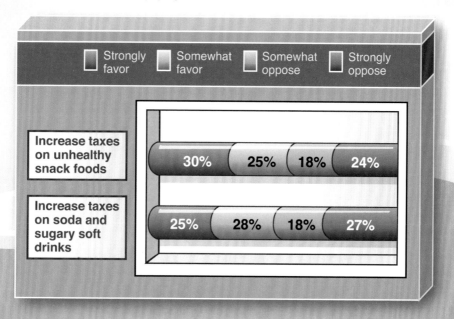

Taken from: Kaiser Family Foundation, July 2009.

If the low "cost" of eating fast food is adding to the obesity problem, the solution involves increasing the cost, even in a nominal way. How do we give individuals the incentive to pay a little more—increased physical exertion, lack of convenience—to get their food? This is where a drive-through tax comes in.

Drive-Through Food Should Be Taxed

We could tax the drive-through purchases at, say, 10 percent, while leaving the purchase of walk-in meals alone. At the very least, it may entice some to park and walk rather than waiting in the car.

Now, this may seem an invasion of personal choice or another step toward a nanny state. Maybe. But there are other arguments to be made. We tax cigarettes in part because of their health cost. Similarly, the individual's decision to lead a sedentary lifestyle will end up costing taxpayers. In 2001, the surgeon general issued a report noting that obesity and its complications cost the nation $117 billion annually, much of it through Medicare and Medicaid.

Fast-Food Taxes Could Pay for Something Worthwhile

Imposing a drive-through tax would be one way of recouping future taxpayer outlays—perhaps revenues could go directly to government health programs. And who knows, it could help the environment, too: with one move, we could fight obesity and reduce emissions from all those cars idling in the line at Burger King.

> **EVALUATING THE AUTHOR'S ARGUMENTS:**
>
> To make his argument, Martin B. Schmidt compares fast food to cigarettes. What is the comparison he makes? Do you think it is valid to compare the two? In what ways are they similar? In what ways are they different?

Viewpoint 4

Fast Food Should Not Be Taxed

Jordan Ballor

"Taxes like the fast food tax are quick fixes that would have serious economic and moral consequences."

In the following viewpoint Jordan Ballor advises against imposing a tax on fast food. He argues that city governments who seek to tax fast food are just looking for easy ways to increase their budgets. They do not really care about discouraging people from eating fast food—in fact, he claims, if they start to profit from fast-food purchases, it would be in their best interest to sell more fast food, not less of it. Ballor also thinks that fast food is not so bad that it needs to be taxed. Many fast-food restaurants offer healthy menu options, he says, and customers could easily avoid the tax by simply going to a fast-food restaurant in a non-taxed region. Ballor concludes that taxing fast food is wrong and hypocritical.

Ballor is associate editor of the *Journal of Markets & Morality*.

AS YOU READ, CONSIDER THE FOLLOWING QUESTIONS:
1. What does the word "gluttonous" mean in the context of the viewpoint?

Jordan Ballor, "The Flawed Fast Food Tax," Acton Institute, May 11, 2005. Reproduced by permission.

2. How many quick-service restaurants have added low-carb options to their menus, according to Ballor?
3. Who is Greg Brenneman, and how does he factor into the author's argument?

As politicians look for new ways to prop up their sagging budgets, Detroit mayor Kwame Kilpatrick is the latest political figure to float the idea of a "fast food tax." If his effort is successful, Detroit would become the first city in the nation to pass an extra tax on quickservice food.

In Kilpatrick's proposed city budget, a 2 percent tax on fast food "means if a Happy Meal costs $2.99, the total cost will be $3.05, with the six cents coming to the city." The *Detroit Free Press* editorial page even does Kilpatrick one better, suggesting that the government "tax take-out food statewide—but by calories, not cost."

Just Another "Sin" Tax

As one of the great examples of the American entrepreneurial spirit, fast food restaurants are under growing threats these days. The fast food tax, or "fat tax," is really the newest incarnation of the age-old "sin" tax. The reasoning is that fast foods, which tend to be higher in calories, fat and cholesterol than other types of food, are unhealthy, and therefore worthy of special government attention.

Sin taxes have a long and checkered American history, with the most common sin taxes on liquor and cigarettes. But recently, other kinds of sin taxes have received attention, since so many governments at all levels are facing fiscal constraints. Some have suggested extra taxes on bars and strip clubs. This fast food tax promises to be much more far-reaching, however, as the National Restaurant Association

> ## FAST FACT
>
> In 1999 the state of Maine enacted a 5.5 percent tax on junk food. Despite the tax, Maine's adult obesity rate doubled from 10 percent to 20 percent during the ten years the tax was in effect.

estimates that domestic quickservice sales reached over $140 billion in 2004.

But why shouldn't the state attempt to promote healthy behavior through taxation? The moniker "sin" tax isn't really appropriate when applied to such things as food and drink. A Christian understanding of stewardship includes taking care of our bodies, but within that mandate is wide scope for prudential judgment concerning how to nourish ourselves and how to enjoy the licit pleasures of creation. As Thomas Aquinas writes, "Gluttony denotes, not any desire of eating and drinking, but an inordinate desire."

The Government Should Not Profit from Bad Behavior

But in this case, it is worth asking which is more gluttonous: the fast food consumers who order combo meals, or the governments, which constantly seek new ways to feed their own insatiable appetites. It's a shame that those who so often lament governmental attempts to "legislate morality" don't find anything wrong with the arbitrary taxation of certain legitimate industries and commodities.

In addition, the state's interest in promoting healthy behavior quickly becomes contradictory when sin taxes are introduced. If such activities really are so harmful, government should not have an economic stake in the continuance of such activities. Indeed, government

© 2005 Wright, The Detroit News, and PoliticalCartoons.com.

The National Restaurant Association reports that two-thirds of fast food restaurants offer low-fat, low-calorie, and low-carb menus.

budgets, in seeking the short-term crutch of sin taxes, can quickly become dependent on them for long-term viability.

Fast Food Is Not the Devil

And the fast food industry is really too easy a target for the government. Besieged by the media and public opinion (consider the popularity of the film *Super Size Me*), quickservice restaurants have gotten the reputation for being extremely unhealthy.

But the truth of the matter is more complex. The National Restaurant Association reports that two-thirds of quickservice restaurants have added low-carb options to their menus. As usual, the service industry responds quickly and efficiently to customer demands.

Burger King CEO [chief executive officer] Greg Brenneman recently said in a *Wall Street Journal* interview that he feels no pressure to respond to critics of the fast food industry. "You should be able to come to Burger King and get a healthy, low-calorie, low-fat meal. You can. Beyond that, I don't think its my job to tell Americans what they should eat. We might as well go back to communism." Have it your way, indeed.

Fast Food Taxes Are a Greedy Idea

Whether Kilpatrick's proposal is approved or not, it will ultimately fail because such a capricious tax on fast food will be met by a corresponding market force. In the words of 18-year-old Ebony Ellis in an AP [Associated Press] report, "Just tell him we're going to go to Bloomfield Hills [a Detroit suburb] to McDonald's if he puts a tax on it."

As a rule, governments should not seek quick and temporary fixes to structural budget problems. Sin taxes like the fast food tax are quick fixes that would have serious economic and moral consequences. Government leaders really ought to address their own appetite for spending tax dollars before they try to regulate the appetites of their constituents.

EVALUATING THE AUTHORS' ARGUMENTS:

Jordan Ballor and Martin A. Schmidt, author of the previous viewpoint, disagree on whether fast food should be taxed. After reading both viewpoints, with which author do you agree? Why? Cite evidence from the texts that helped you form your opinion.

Chapter 3

How Should Fast Food Be Marketed?

The McDonald's Corporation has used the clown Ronald McDonald as a marketing tool to appeal to children since the 1960s.

Fast-Food Restaurants Should Have to Post Nutritional Information

Hannah Pingree

"Consumers often choose to eat less or make different choices about what they eat when they have basic calorie information."

In the following viewpoint Hannah Pingree explains why she thinks fast-food restaurants should be required to post nutritional information about their food. Without such information, Pingree says, people have no clear idea of how many calories are in their food. She points to one study that found Americans drastically underestimated the amount of calories in fast food—the dish in question had nearly twice the amount of calories people guessed it did. Pingree says this is proof that people need help understanding how many calories are in their food. When they understand the nutritional consequences of their choices, they will be better equipped to avoid diabetes, obesity, and other diseases. To this

Hannah Pingree, "Put Fast-Food Calorie Content in Consumers' Hands," bangordailynews.com, March 10, 2009. Reproduced by permission of Bangor Daily News.

end, Pingree says fast-food restaurants should have to post nutritional information about their food.

Pingree is the speaker of the Maine House of Representatives. She supports legislation that would require fast-food companies to increase customer access to nutritional information.

AS YOU READ, CONSIDER THE FOLLOWING QUESTIONS:
1. According to the author, what is Maine's definition of a chain restaurant?
2. How many calories does Pingree say people guessed were in a typical hamburger and onion rings? How many calories are *actually* in a hamburger and onion rings?
3. What is the Nutrition Labeling and Education Act of 1990, as described by Pingree?

We've all been there.

You're late for an appointment and breakfast is a distant memory. If you don't get lunch, you'll listen to your rumbling stomach for hours. You're trying to keep your New Year's resolution to eat more healthfully, but you only have five minutes to spare and you can't eat a salad while driving.

How does a spicy chicken sandwich with mayo and a soda fit into your goal of keeping your caloric intake around 2,000 calories per day? How many more calories if you add the small fries? How many calories are in the kids meal? Which has more calories, the tuna salad sandwich or the roast beef sandwich? How can you make a healthful lunch choice while still keeping that appointment?

People Need Help Avoiding Obesity and Disease

Every day, countless Mainers face this scenario. The convenience that fast food provides is undeniable, but, unfortunately, so is the increasing effect of obesity on the lives of Mainers. And we know that fast food is a key contributor to increasing waistlines and declining health.

This year [2009] we are proposing a common sense law requiring national chain restaurants in Maine to post calorie contents on their menus. (A chain is defined as any Maine restaurant that has 15 or more locations nationally.) This legislation will provide essential health information to help all of us make more informed choices. It will promote greater transparency for consumers.

We know that being overweight and obese results in higher rates of chronic disease, which negatively affects Mainers' quality of life and increases health care costs. Currently, two-thirds of Maine adults are either overweight or obese—a rate that has doubled in the past 15 years. Obesity is associated with multiple health problems, including cardiovascular disease, diabetes, asthma, and arthritis.

McDonald's director of nutrition displays the new nutrition label the company will display on its packaging.

Nutritional Information Is Not Obvious

Nationally, both mandatory and voluntary programs that place calorie content on menu boards at restaurants have been shown to positively affect choices made by consumers. Consumers often choose to eat less or make different choices about what they eat when they have basic calorie information.

Without nutritional information, many don't know that a tuna salad sandwich from a typical deli has 720 calories compared to a roast beef sandwich with mustard, which has only 460 calories. Even trained nutritionists cannot make accurate estimates. According to a study by the Center for Science in the Public Interest, when shown a typical hamburger and onion rings, dietitians on average estimated that it had 865 calories, when it actually contained 1,550 calories.

Restaurants Should Post Information Nationally

Last year [2008], New York City implemented the first menu labeling law that applied to chain restaurants. Since then, the state of California and cities such as Portland, Ore., and Philadelphia have followed suit. Massachusetts is reviewing rules to apply the policy to the entire state.

This approach clearly has momentum. National companies, such as McDonald's and Chili's, are providing the information on their menu boards in New York City—a city of 8 million people and thousands of restaurants, and they will soon be doing the same in California. They should provide the same information to their customers here in Maine.

Like Groceries, Fast Food Should Be Labeled

The federal Nutrition Labeling and Education Act of 1990 requires food labeling on almost all packaged foods sold at supermarkets, con-

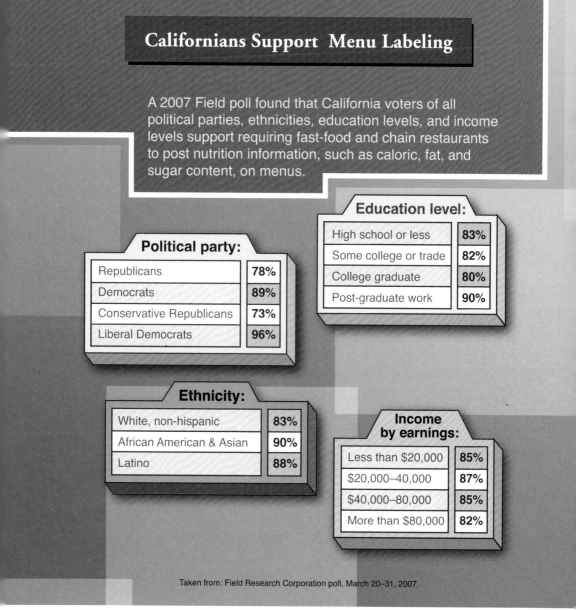

Californians Support Menu Labeling

A 2007 Field poll found that California voters of all political parties, ethnicities, education levels, and income levels support requiring fast-food and chain restaurants to post nutrition information, such as caloric, fat, and sugar content, on menus.

Education level:

High school or less	83%
Some college or trade	82%
College graduate	80%
Post-graduate work	90%

Political party:

Republicans	78%
Democrats	89%
Conservative Republicans	73%
Liberal Democrats	96%

Ethnicity:

White, non-hispanic	83%
African American & Asian	90%
Latino	88%

Income by earnings:

Less than $20,000	85%
$20,000–40,000	87%
$40,000–80,000	85%
More than $80,000	82%

Taken from: Field Research Corporation poll, March 20–31, 2007.

venience stores, and other retail stores. About half of people report that the nutrition information on food labels has caused them to change their minds about buying a food product, according to a study by the Food and Drug Administration.

Whether you are dieting or just like to compare products, the information we've all had for nearly 18 years in the grocery store has helped Maine consumers make decisions. It hasn't forced choices or told people what to eat—but provided them with basic health data.

Our proposal aims to do the same thing in Maine for those restaurants that have both regular formula menus and have, for the most part, already successfully complied with this law in other parts of the country.

Obesity and poor nutrition affect everyone in Maine. They increase the overall health care costs we all pay and affect the health and welfare of our kids, families, friends and neighbors. Putting basic information in the hands of consumers will allow us all to take the lead in improving our health and the health of our kids and families.

EVALUATING THE AUTHOR'S ARGUMENTS:

In this viewpoint Hannah Pingree uses facts and examples to make her argument that fast-food restaurants should have to post nutritional information. She does not, however, use any quotations to support her points. If you were to rewrite this article and insert quotations, what authorities might you quote from? Where would you place these quotations to bolster the points Pingree makes?

Fast-Food Restaurants Should Not Have to Post Nutritional Information

"The vast majority of people who eat in fast-food restaurants are not going to choose their dinner based on how many calories it contains."

Rob Lyons

The government should not force fast-food restaurants to post the nutritional content of their dishes, argues Rob Lyons in the following viewpoint. The main reason Lyons opposes mandatory nutritional postings is that he thinks they will not make a difference in what people eat. He says people eat fast food because it tastes good, not because they care how many calories are in it. Since most people are bound to ignore nutritional postings, he sees little point in requiring them to be posted. Lyons also says it is wrong to make people think that all they need to do to lose weight is count calories. He says weight loss is a complicated endeavor that will not be accomplished by forcing fast-food companies to post information about their food.

Rob Lyons, "Calorie-Counting Is an Eating Disorder," *Spiked,* April 8, 2009. Reproduced by permission.

All the postings will do, in Lyons's opinion, is rob people of their right to enjoy a guilty pleasure.

Lyons is deputy editor of the online magazine *Spiked,* in which this viewpoint was originally published.

AS YOU READ, CONSIDER THE FOLLOWING QUESTIONS:
1. According to Lyons, why do people love fast food?
2. How many fewer calories does Lyons say New Yorkers consumed after they learned the nutritional content of their fast-food meals?
3. According to Lyons, what is the difference in life expectancy between people of normal weight and people who are mildly obese?

Big Mac: 500. Regular fries: 250 or so. Diet soda: zero . . . Total: 750-ish; 1,250 left for today.

Welcome to the world of calorie counting.

This is the kind of nutritional accountancy that our health guardians would like all of us to undertake every day. Now, some of the UK's [United Kingdom's] biggest restaurant chains will be joining in the fun by prominently displaying the calorie content of their menu items. And it's not just the usual 'ethical' suspects like [stores] Marks and Spencer or Waitrose; fast-food joints like Pizza Hut and KFC [Kentucky Fried Chicken] and big workplace caterers like Compass and Sodexo are also jumping on the calorie bandwagon.

The March Toward Mandatory Calorie Counting

According to the UK Food Standards Agency (FSA), who together with the UK Department of Health came up with the idea that we should always be told how many calories we are consuming, by June [2009] more than 450 food outlets across Britain will have introduced calorie information, some on a pilot basis. Each company will 'display calorie information for most food and drink they serve, print calorie information on menu boards, paper menus or on the edge of shelves, and ensure the information is clear and easily visible at the point where people choose their food'.

The UK minister for public health Dawn Primarolo, announcing the first batch of 18 companies taking part in the scheme, said: 'We know that people want to be able to see how many calories are in the food and drink they order when they eat out. I want to see more catering companies join this ground-breaking first group to help their customers make healthier choices.'

For the moment, the scheme is voluntary, but it isn't hard to imagine it becoming compulsory, if it takes off and is judged a 'success'. That is already the situation in New York, where the city authorities imposed a requirement on chain restaurants to display nutritional information from March 2008. A similar idea was floated in Australia in January [2009].

Customers Do Not Care What Is in Their Fast Food

An obvious criticism of these schemes is that they are unlikely to make much difference. While those who are on a perpetual diet (mostly women) might modify their eating-out choices when presented with

Critics of requiring nutrition labels for fast food maintain that such labels may well be useless, saying that those who eat at fast-food restaurants are unlikely to be interested in such information.

nutritional information, the vast majority of people who eat in fast-food restaurants are not going to choose their dinner based on how many calories it contains.

For all the token efforts of McDonald's and others to present themselves in a healthier light, fast food is about fat, sugar and salt in the kind of quantities that induce apoplexy amongst our health guardians. That's why we love it. Even when the companies themselves aren't tempting us with supersized mega-burgers, customers 'pimp' the meals themselves: try trapping a McDonald's chicken burger *inside* a cheeseburger for a two-dollar treat tastefully known as a 'McGangBang'.

Moreover, even if these policies did manage to reduce our calorie intake, such cuts would be unlikely to make any difference to our waistlines. The experience from New York seems to be that diners consumed between 50 and 100 fewer calories per meal after the labelling rules came in. Given that a pound of solid fat contains around 4,000 calories, a simple back-of-a-burger-box calculation suggests it could take anything between 40 and 80 trips to your local chain for these labels to produce a single pound of weight loss. And that's assuming that punters [customers] don't reward their newfound restraint in restaurants by having a chocolate bar when they get home.

Weight Loss Is More than Just Counting Calories

The whole business of weight loss is much more complicated than these schemes suggest. Calorie-controlled diets have a high failure rate. Most people who lose a substantial amount of weight pile it back on again over subsequent months or—at best—years. Nor is carrying a few extra pounds the death sentence it is often presented as; in fact, there is almost no difference in life expectancy between those of 'nor-

© 2005 John Trever, The Albuquerque Journal and PoliticalCartoons.com.

mal' weight and those who are labelled 'mildly obese'. Even amongst those who really are grossly overweight, the relationship between food intake, weight and ill-health is more complex than people assume.

Indeed, as Morgan Spurlock discovered in his film *Super Size Me*, overeating is, for most people, quite hard work. You don't need a calorie counter to tell you when you've grossed out. So why do some people feel satisfied with hamster-sized portions, while others aren't happy unless they 'go large'? Why do some fail to gain weight on a diet of lard-sodden burgers while others restrain themselves and can't shift the weight? It's a tricky, multi-faceted business, obesity. Reducing the problem to a matter of calories—just one aspect of the food we eat—hasn't solved the 'problem' of growing waistlines in the past two or three decades, and it won't solve it any time soon.

Labels Rob Us of the Joy of Eating

But even if this new policy were successful at shifting weight, encouraging an outbreak of obsessive calorie-counting disorder is a bad idea in itself. Food should be both sustenance *and* pleasure. The demand that we constantly check our desires against some government-imposed calorie-related target robs us of this joy, replacing it with guilt and fear instead; such schemes serve no other purpose than to persuade us that we must trust in the advice of the health authorities.

Rather than labelling everything we eat with calorie and fat contents, a far healthier attitude would be to leave us to make up our own minds about what we consume. We should be lickin' our fingers, not counting calories on them.

EVALUATING THE AUTHORS' ARGUMENTS:

Rob Lyons says that requiring fast-food companies to post nutritional information is pointless because very few customers are going to change what they order based on it. How do you think Hannah Pingree, author of the previous viewpoint, would respond to this claim? Use specific evidence from the texts in your answer.

Fast-Food Ads Should Be Banned

Mark Morford

"Is this still legal? Do we still actually allow this sort of cultural tripe to be broadcast to the nation?"

In the following viewpoint Mark Morford argues that fast-food advertisements should have limits. He describes a commercial for a Wendy's product called the "Baconator," a fat-filled double cheeseburger piled with six strips of bacon. He says such advertising is wrong because it shamelessly tries to push a product that is clearly unhealthy. He rejects the suggestion that it is people's responsibility to avoid fast food, pointing out that the government passes other laws to protect people from harmful substances such as alcohol or tobacco. Morford concludes that nothing is wrong with limiting the extent to which harmful products can be advertised to the nation.

Morford is a columnist for the *San Francisco Chronicle*.

AS YOU READ, CONSIDER THE FOLLOWING QUESTIONS:

1. Describe the Wendy's commercial for the Baconator and explain what the author finds offensive about it.
2. What, according to Morford, is the target audience for most fast-food ads?
3. What does Morford think should "not be allowed free reign" in American culture?

Mark Morford, "Eat This, You Fat, Sad Idiot," SFGate.com, September 19, 2007. Reproduced by permission.

I admit scattershot naivete. I admit to a strain of blind optimism, a sort of sporadic myopia, a weirdly sanguine tunnel vision that makes me somehow think that we as a species and a culture and as a mad gaggle of individual human souls who are coupled with functioning hunks of semi-rational gray matter, we must, at least occasionally, be learning something, ever-so-slightly advancing our awareness of those things on this planet that want to harm us and sicken us and even kill us, and therefore we can alter our behaviors accordingly.

Fast-Food Ads Are Getting Worse

I must be completely wrong. Because there it is, that violently obnoxious Wendy's burger commercial I stumbled across recently, apparently part of a larger and stranger ad campaign featuring the usual assortment of requisite sagging thick-waisted former frat dudes—a group, by the way, that must be an entire category unto itself for Los Angeles casting agencies, given how many of them appear in all sorts of similar monosyllabic commercials for, say, trucks. Or beer. Or power tools. Et al.

These ads feature the same childish concept: All the dudes have bright red cartoon pigtails (a la the Wendy's mascot) where their receding hairline used to be, and in their thick fists they're maybe clutching a giant greasy burger and staring at it with a sort of desperate, animalistic lust you normally see from, say, secretly gay Idaho Republicans in airport restrooms. Or something.

But this particular ad offers something extra, something a bit more . . . extraordinary. The burger in question is something very special indeed. It is not your typical "value menu" item. It is not a Wendy's Single with Cheese, or whatever it's called down in noncomestible junk-food hell.

A Wholly Offensive Product

No, this insidious concoction is simply startling in its shameless toxicity, its ruthless attention to wanting you cancerous and morbidly obese and very, very dead as soon as goddamn possible, if not sooner.

The burger is this: two sickeningly brownish-gray, chemical-blasted 1/4-pound beeflike patties, intersliced with two slabs of neon-orange cheeselike substance, slathered with mayonnaise, all topped with the big kicker: six (yes, six) strips of bacon. Oh my, yes. It's like a giant middle finger to your heart.

This product's name? The "Baconator." You know, like "Terminator," only for, uh, a huge stack of cow/pig meat that celebrates your impending coronary/impotence/cancer with every bite. Genius.

Why Are Such Ads Not Illegal?

Here is where I admit my confusion. Here is where a small but significant part of my brain (quietly, internally) explodes every time I see this commercial—which, mercifully, isn't often, because I don't watch much TV and don't watch any weekend TV sports and therefore am never around when (I presume) this kind of product is target-marketed straight to their apparently very slovenly, apparently hugely unhealthy, largely illiterate audiences.

Wait, is that too harsh? Maybe. But as I watched this ad, a slew of questions flooded my naive brain and I found myself actually looking around my apartment, trying to find a sympathetic face, someone or something to share my stupefaction at what I was seeing. Wait wait wait (I asked the wall), is this still legal? Do we still actually allow

On a bun slathered in mayonnaise, Wendy's "Baconator" is piled high with two quarter-pound beef patties, two slabs of processed cheese, and six pieces of bacon.

this sort of cultural tripe to be broadcast to the nation? Can fast-food companies still sell revolting chyme [partially digested stomach contents] like this obesity-causing cancer-ready death-inducing product you shouldn't even feed to your dog, and no one is stopping them? Didn't we pass a law or something? Have the noxious fast-food titans not yet been forced to stop concocting vile products like this, or at least to dial down the garish marketing of their most ultra-toxic products, given how the vast majority of Americans have now learned (haven't they?) at least a tiny modicum about human health?

Put another, more pointed way: Haven't we moved past this by now?

Fast-Food Companies Would Happily Hurt Us

After all, we've now had years—decades, even—of well-documented studies and health campaigns and even a handful of truth-in-advertising nutrition laws, endless media reports about the dangers of fat and chemicals and industrial feedlot beef, not to mention the launch of dozens of health magazines and the mixed-blessing triumph of the entire organic movement, right alongside pop culture hits like "Fast Food Nation" and "Super Size Me" and "The Omnivore's Dilemma" and "Diet for a New America" and all the rest.

Hence, you'd think—or at least, I thought—something might have shifted by now. Alas, you would be, like me, completely wrong.

Yes, well do I know the brutish libertarian view of all this, which simply goes: If you're dumb enough to eat this garbage, you get what you deserve. Then again, such ideology doesn't stop us from passing laws—or at least partially regulating—vile corporations and products we know are hugely dangerous and stupid and which would happily kill us in our sleep. And, at least in some cases, we're better off for it.

The Government Routinely Protects Its Citizens

Hell, we did it with telemarketing. One little much-needed law and boom, a national Do-Not-Call registry, and it actually mostly works and now all those vile cretins who used to call you during dinner to sell you carpet cleaning services now simply spare your e-mail account until it staggers and collapses and shuts down your e-mail server. Yay!

We did it with cigarette advertising, with booze, with seat belt laws, with gun advertising, with all sorts of products and services we know in our collective heart of hearts are either totally and shamelessly deadly and therefore should not be allowed free reign in the culture, or which we all agree really do need some sort of system of legal/ethical checks and balances (clean water, food additives, medicine, etc.) that the free market simply cannot provide on its own.

Hoping for a Smarter, Safer America

And yes, well do I know the cynical view, the one that says a law banning the creation or advertising of such deadly garbage like the Baconator probably wouldn't do much to stem the tide of willful ignorance in this country anyway, given our well-known epidemic of obesity and our proud, all-American culture of gluttony and excess. True enough.

But maybe I'll just stick with my original note of (blind?) confidence, that little bubble of ideological hope that progress has indeed been made and awareness of health and diet in this nation has indeed been nicely raised and the world is not, in fact, teeming with an army of manic Baconator-chomping frat guys.

Or better yet, maybe I should just stop watching TV altogether. Voila! No more Baconators! Easy.

> ## EVALUATING THE AUTHOR'S ARGUMENTS:
>
> Mark Morford compares fast food to guns, alcohol, and cigarettes. He says that advertisements for these products have been restricted and so too should fast food advertisements. What do you think—does fast food belong in the same category as guns, alcohol, and cigarettes? Why or why not?

Fast-Food Ads Should Not Be Banned

Sandy Sand

"Banning advertising by legal, legitimate enterprises is not the way to get people to become svelte, or to live a lifetime of healthful eating."

Banning fast-food ads is the wrong response to the nation's obesity problem, argues Sandy Sand in the following viewpoint. She says that fast food has a useful place in American culture, and as such, companies have the right to advertise their product. If parents do not want their kids to be overexposed to such ads, Sand suggests not letting them watch as much television, which is bad for them anyway. Finally, Sand warns that limiting fast-food ads would hurt the economy by cutting off valuable fast-food advertising dollars and threatening hundreds of thousands of jobs. For all of these reasons, Sand says that fast-food ads should not be limited.

Sand is a columnist for the *Los Angeles Daily News* and a contributor to ronkayela .com.

AS YOU READ, CONSIDER THE FOLLOWING QUESTIONS:

1. Who does Sand speculate may have been the driving force behind a National Bureau of Economic Research study about childhood obesity?

Sandy Sand, "The Fanatical Food Fascists Are at it Again," Salon.com, November 22, 2008. This article first appeared in Salon.com, at www.salon.com. An online version remains in the Salon archives. Reprinted with permission of the author.

2. What two actions other than banning fast-food ads does the author say would more effectively get Americans to eat healthier?
3. What does Sand say would be more unhealthy for fast-food workers than eating the product that they make?

They want to ban advertising fast food on television.

Fast Food Exists Because People Need It

You want to control what people eat and stop so many from becoming the unsightly fatties of the world? Start teaching home-ec classes in kindergarten for both boys and girls and hang pictures of Twiggy on all the walls, but don't ban fast food ads.

Fast food is the staple of a huge number of Americans' diets. If it weren't, all the fast food places would have gone in the garbage disposal long ago.

Speeding up to the drive-thru is a way of life for many parents, both of whom might be holding down more than one job just to keep body and soul together.

Fat Kids Are the Parents' Fault

If the fanatical we-know-what's-good-for-you-but-you-don't fast food fascists get their way fast food ads will be banned from television.

In a report by economists at the National Bureau of Economic Research, and published in the *Journal of Law & Economics*, on Nov. 20th [2008], kids—aged six through 11—have gotten fatter by 13% since 1970, because they watch television with fast food–laden commercials for hours on end. . . .

Isn't that more or less the bottom line?

Some people argue that advertising by fast-food chains is not to blame for the obesity epidemic among children. Rather, they say, it is the fault of parents who persist in feeding their children fast food and who also fail to encourage them to exercise.

It's not the fast food ads that are driving them through the drive-thru that's making them fat, it's parents whose means to the end of feeding them is fast food. It's the fault of those same parents who allow their children to sit on their asses watching the TV all day instead of going outside to play, and who drive them up to fast food take-out windows.

What People Eat Is a Personal Choice

First, I always want to know who paid for this or any study.

In this case, was it the lean meat chicken people? Vegans? The leaner other white meat people? Self-loathing fatties? Or a bunch of freakin' busy body control freaks, who have nothing better to do with their time than tell us how we should eat?

Second, I was never a fast food freak, and rarely zipped through the drive-thru on my way home from work so I could throw any kind of food at my kids. Either I made dinner before leaving the house or when I got home, or called them from my desk and told them how to start preparing dinner.

It wasn't that hard to do, nor did it make me a saint for doing it. It was just the way it was, and I didn't feel particularly burdened by the task of providing them with a reasonably wholesome meal at the end of the day.

Healthy Eating Habits Cannot Be Mandated

Banning advertising by legal, legitimate enterprises is not the way to get people to become svelte, or to live a lifetime of healthful eating.

Education from an early age is part of the answer. Getting McDonald's, Carl's Jr, Taco Bell and the hundreds of other fast food

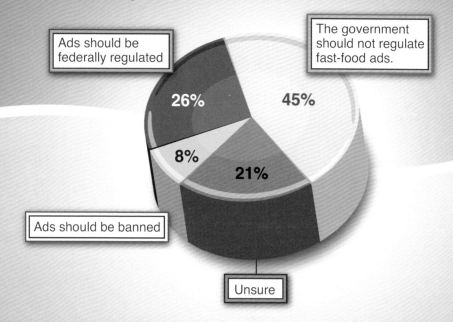

Americans Do Not Think Fast-Food Ads Should Be Limited

A 2009 poll found that on the whole, Americans think it is wrong to limit or regulate advertisements for fast food and junk food.

Ads should be federally regulated — 26%

The government should not regulate fast-food ads. — 45%

Ads should be banned — 8%

Unsure — 21%

Taken from: AdweekMedia/Harris poll, July 2009.

chains to voluntarily co-operate and reduce the calories in their meals is another way.

Of course, that would also make their food more expensive, because they'd be forced to stop using fillers and to use higher grade, lower fat content meat in their burgers, or switch to turkey burgers, which are totally disgusting and unpalatable unless they're drowned in an ocean of condiments.

Banning Fast Food Ads Hurts the Economy

For all practical purposes, during our current economic crisis this is not the time to be talking about banning advertising for multi-million-billion dollar businesses that employ hundreds of thousands of unskilled workers. Being out of a job would be far more unhealthful for them and the economy in general than eating the food at their work places.

My bottom line for these interferers is butt out! Stop trying to legislate healthful eating habits and healthful living, because it won't work. You're burning up the calories you ingest on a fruitless venture.

And, by the way. Fess up. How often do you patronize your local drive-thru on your way home from an exhausting day at work? Huh?

EVALUATING THE AUTHOR'S ARGUMENTS:

In this viewpoint Sandy Sand takes a blunt, humor-filled approach to making her argument that fast-food advertisements should not be restricted. She does not, however, use statistics and factual details to support her points. Do you think her approach is persuasive? If you were to rewrite this article and insert statistics, where would you place them to bolster the points Sand makes?

Children's Exposure to Fast-Food Ads Should Be Limited

Daniel H. Rasolt

"This form of advertising plays an enormous role in obesity numbers, especially in children."

Reducing children's exposure to fast-food ads has many benefits, argues Daniel H. Rasolt in the following viewpoint. He discusses the findings of a study showing that childhood obesity rates would drop dramatically if children's exposure to fast-food ads were limited. Rasolt accuses fast-food companies of targeting children—even though children themselves have no money, fast-food companies hope to hook customers on their products when they are young and keep them for life. Rasolt thinks this practice is predatory, especially when it comes at the expense of young Americans' health. He realizes that it will be difficult to ban fast-food ads entirely but points out that even proposals to reduce fast-food advertising would have an impact on Americans' health.

Rasolt is a writer for *Defeat Diabetes News,* where this viewpoint was originally published.

AS YOU READ, CONSIDER THE FOLLOWING QUESTIONS:

1. How much does the author say obesity rates would drop in three-to eleven-year-olds if fast-food advertisements were banned?
2. Who does the author say are more susceptible to fast-food ads—boys or girls?
3. What countries have already banned fast-food ads, according to the author? What has been their experience?

Obesity is an epidemic, and its rapid rise has closely coincided with the growth of the so-called "fast-food culture." It's been hotly debated for many years whether fast food advertisements, which are primarily aimed at children in the United States, are in large part responsible for rising obesity levels. A new study, the most comprehensive of its kind, has concluded that indeed this form of advertising plays an enormous role in obesity numbers, especially in children.

Companies Want Young Customers

It's a common belief in many industries that instilling a comfort and recognition of a certain product at a very young age will create a lifelong customer. This is the fundamental reason for the abundance of advertisements aimed at children, who themselves have no purchasing power, and the creation of the famous Joe Camels and Ronald McDonalds of the world. Given that certain products, such as the majority of fast foods, have potentially profound effects on the health of the consumer, getting kids hooked on the food might be partially responsible for rising obesity, and related conditions (heart disease, diabetes, kidney disease, to name a few).

The Benefits of Reducing Kids' Exposure to Fast-Food Ads

The study in question, conducted by the National Bureau of Economic Research (NBER), looked at the potential impact of a ban on fast-food advertising during children's programming. For children 3–11 years of age, researchers concluded that obesity levels would drop by 18%, while in 12–18 year old kids, obesity would drop by 14%. It's also noted that males appear to be more easily influenced by fast-food advertising, so the reduction in obesity due to the ban is more pronounced in male children. The study looked at comprehensive data of more than 13,000 American children, which accounted for their states of health, lifestyle, and "viewing habits."

On the surface, this proposed ban, besides angering the fast-food conglomerates, seems like a near necessity in protecting the nation's children. Unfortunately, there are many deep issues that need to be

Studies have shown that teenage males are more susceptible to fast-food advertising than their female counterparts.

accounted for when considering such measures. The most evident is that the federal government would be essentially interfering with the "free-market" in order to protect children. Many, even outside of the obvious ones with direct incentives, value the guiding capitalistic principles that America's economy is supposed to be built on, above all else. Too much government involvement is a scary possibility for these people.

It Has Worked in Other Countries

Thankfully, there is already a precedent for similar policies, as similar restrictions have been implemented in other countries. The Scandinavian countries, Norway, Sweden and Finland, pioneered the bans on advertising during children's programming, which coincided with declining child-obesity rates in those countries. While these countries don't have the same aversion to big government that many Americans do, at least they provide evidence that the ban really can work.

While it wasn't of primary focus in the study, another interesting proposal and conclusion was drawn regarding the elimination of tax-deductible food advertisements. Business expenses are non-taxable, and food advertisements are now considered a business expense. Making the money used for advertisements taxable, the researchers suggest, would decrease fast-food advertising aimed at children by 40%, and 33% for that aimed at adolescents. Specifically, food advertising would cost 54% more if it was no longer tax-deductible. It's suggested that this would then translate to a 5–7% decrease in obesity levels in children.

> **FAST FACT**
>
> A study published in the January 30, 2009, issue of the *International Journal of Behavioral Nutrition and Physical Activity* found that high school students who watched more than five hours of television a day ate more fast food, fried food, and sugary drinks. Heavy-TV-viewing adolescents consumed about two hundred more calories per day than moderate TV viewers.

Children See Many Ads for Fast Food and Junk Food

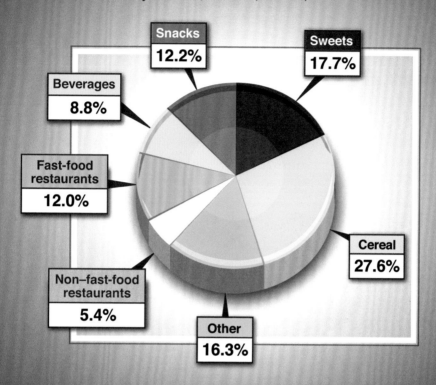

About 80 percent of advertising targeted at children is for unhealthy sweets, snacks, cereal, and fast food.

Snacks
12.2%

Sweets
17.7%

Beverages
8.8%

Fast-food restaurants
12.0%

Cereal
27.6%

Non–fast-food restaurants
5.4%

Other
16.3%

Taken from: *Archives of Pediatric and Adolescent Medicine*, "Exposure to Food Advertising on Television Among U.S. Children," June 2007.

An Easy Way to Reduce Childhood Obesity

Childhood obesity has become a major problem in the United States, with 10–15% of young children and adolescents being at least significantly overweight. This study also notes that an overweight child has more than an 80% chance of becoming an obese adult, and obese adults have a much higher incidence of numerous life-threatening conditions. In fact, in the United States alone, obesity is thought to be responsible (directly and indirectly) for more than 300,000 deaths per year. Not all of this can be blamed on advertising fatty foods to kids, but following this study, it's hard to deny that it plays a role. Study author Dr. Shin-Yi Chou eyes [sic] an impact: "Hopefully, this line of research can lead to a serious discussion about the type of policies that can curb America's obesity epidemic."

EVALUATING THE AUTHOR'S ARGUMENTS:

Daniel H. Rasolt discusses the ways in which children are particularly prone to fast-food advertisements. His solution is to ban them. What do you think—should fast-food ads be banned? In your answer, list at least two positive outcomes and two negative outcomes from such a ban. Then, state your ultimate opinion on the matter.

Facts About Fast Food

Editor's note: These facts can be used in reports or papers to reinforce or add credibility when making important points or claims.

Fast-Food Consumption in America

According to the *Encyclopedia of Junk Food and Fast Food*:

- In 1970 Americans spent about $6 billion a year on fast food. By 2006 Americans were spending nearly $142 billion.
- There are more than 300,000 fast-food restaurants in the United States.
- French fries are the single most popular fast food in America.
- In 1970 french fries surpassed regular potato sales in the United States.
- McDonald's is the largest purchaser of beef, pork, and potatoes, and the second largest purchaser of chicken, in the world.
- By the end of the twentieth century, one in eight American workers had at some time been employed by McDonald's.
- 96 percent of Americans have been to a McDonald's at least once.

According to the Super Size Me Web site, as of 2009:

- Each day, one in four Americans visits a fast-food restaurant.
- A person would have to walk for seven hours straight to burn off a supersized Coke, french fries, and Big Mac.
- More than 1 million animals are eaten per hour in the United States.
- Forty percent of American meals are eaten outside the home.
- McDonald's represents 43 percent of the total U.S. fast-food market.

Fast food is now served at restaurants and drive-throughs, at stadiums, airports, zoos, high schools, elementary schools, and universities, on cruise ships, trains, and airplanes, at Kmarts, Walmarts, gas stations, and even at hospital cafeterias, according to Eric Schlosser, the author of *Fast Food Nation.*

Globalization of Fast Food

According to the McDonald's Corporation:

- As of 2008, more than 31,000 restaurants existed in 119 countries.
- Nearly 47 million customers worldwide are served at McDonald's restaurants each day.
- McDonald's employs more than 1.5 million people.
- On January 31, 1990, McDonald's opened a restaurant in Moscow and broke opening-day records for the number of customers served. The Moscow restaurant is the busiest in the world.
- The largest McDonald's in the world is located in Beijing, China.
- McDonald's is the largest employer in Brazil.

In 2006 the global fast-food market grew by 4.8 percent and reached a value of $102.4 billion, according to the company Research and Markets.

According to Worldwatch Institute, the fast-food industry is growing 40 percent each year in India.

Burger King has more than 11,100 restaurants in more than sixty-five countries, according to its Web site.

According to its Web site, Kentucky Fried Chicken (KFC) can be found in twenty-five countries.

As of May 2009, Subway had approximately 31,129 restaurants in ninety countries, making it one of the fastest-growing franchises in the world.

According to its Web site, Pizza Hut is located in twenty-six countries, with one hundred locations in China.

Taco Bell has 278 restaurants located in twelve countries besides the United States.

Fast Food and Advertising

In 2005 *Advertising Age* cited Ronald McDonald as the number two advertising icon of the twentieth century. The Marlboro Man was number one.

Today the average child sees more than ten thousand food advertisements each year on television, according to the book *McDonaldization of Society 5.*

According to taxfastfood.com, food companies spend more than $10 billion each year paying graphic designers and advertising and marketing executives to make their food look delicious and alluring.

Facts About Fast Food, Nutrition, and Health

According to the Tufts University nutrition department:

- Most teenagers need about 2,000 calories a day, depending on their age and activity levels.
- A McDonald's meal consisting of a Big Mac, large fries, and large Coke yields 1,350 calories. It is high in protein, iron, fat, cholesterol, sodium, and sugar.

According to the Calorie King for Food Awareness Web site:

- Proportionally, hash browns have more fat and calories than a cheeseburger or Big Mac.
- Burger King's Double Whopper with cheese contains 923 calories. A man would need to walk for about nine miles to burn it off. Adding french fries and a large cola brings the total to 1,500 calories, which is two-thirds of an adult man's recommended daily caloric intake.
- A small packet of Wendy's honey mustard dressing has 280 calories.

The American Heart Association recommends that people eat no more than a maximum of 2 grams of trans fat per day, 1,000–3,000 milligrams of sodium, and 44–66 grams of fat.

According to the British Broadcasting Corporation one meal from Pizza Hut contains four times the daily limit of salt for a six-year old.

According to FoxNews.com, a June 2008 ban on trans fats in New York City has caused some fast-food restaurants to change their recipes. Menu overhauls at major chains include:

- Dunkin' Donuts: Stopped using partially hydrogenated oil; switched to a trans-fat-free blend of palm, soybean, and cottonseed oils.
- KFC: Removed trans fats from cooking oil, its potpies, and biscuits.
- Pizza Hut: Removed trans fats from the one style of pizza that had it.
- McDonald's: Stopped cooking french fries in trans fats. Eliminated trans fats from cookies and baked apple pies, at least those served in the New York area. The chain has plans to make the change nationwide.
- Burger King: New York restaurants no longer use trans fat to make french fries, apple pie, or biscuits. The chain has plans to make the change nationwide.

According to a 2009 study about posting nutritional information in fast-food restaurants reported in the journal *Health Affairs*:

- A little more than half of the customers noticed the calorie postings.
- Despite this, only 28 percent said the information influenced their order.
- After labels were posted, the amount of saturated fat, sodium, or sugar purchased did not decrease.

A 2007 *American Journal of Clinical Nutrition* study found that weekly consumption of fast food by adolescents is associated with a 0.2 unit increase in BMI (body mass index).

Fast Food and Disease

According to *Fast Food and the Supersizing of America*, several fast-food ingredients have been linked to various cancers, diseases, and/or obesity. These include:

- monosodium glutamate (MSG)
- trans fat
- sodium nitrite
- butylated hydroxyanisole (BHA)

- butylated hydroxytoluene (BHT)
- propyl gallate
- aspartame
- acesulfame-K
- olestra
- potassium bromate
- food coloring blue 1 and 2, red 3, green 3, and yellow 6

According to the Centers for Disease Control and Prevention:
- About a third of American kids are overweight or obese.
- America's obesity rates increased from 18 percent in 1998 to 25 percent in 2006.
- The cost of providing treatment for those patients' weight-driven problems increased health care spending by $40 billion a year.
- Approximately 248,000 Americans die prematurely due to obesity.
- Obesity is the number two cause of preventable death in the United States (smoking is the first).

Eating fast food can result in high levels of insulin, which has been linked to rising incidences of type 2 diabetes. In fact, more than 600,000 new cases of diabetes are diagnosed each year, according to *Fast Food and the Supersizing of America.*

According to an obesity researcher from Boston's Children's Hospital:
- In 1970 fast food accounted for less than 2 percent of the caloric intake of children.
- By the early 1990s it accounted for more than 10 percent.
- Today, children receive 38 percent of their energy from fast food.

Fast Food and Taxes

According to an Urban Institute study on obesity, a 10 percent tax on fattening foods would yield more than $500 billion in revenue over ten years.

A 2006 Centers for Disease Control and Prevention study found that forty U.S. states impose modest additional sales taxes on soft drinks and a few snack items.

According to a June 2009 Kaiser Family Foundation poll:

- Fifty-three percent of Americans favor an increased tax on sodas and other sugary drinks to help pay for health care reform.
- Among those who oppose the idea, 63 percent said they would switch their stance if it raised money for reform while also tackling the problems that stem from obesity.

American Opinions About Fast Food

According to the 2009 Restaurant Industry Forecast:

- Sixty-eight percent of adults said their favorite restaurant foods provide flavors that cannot be easily duplicated at home;
- 76 percent of adults said they are currently trying to eat healthier at restaurants than they did two years ago;
- 70 percent of adults said they were more likely to visit a restaurant that offers locally produced food items;
- 69 percent of adults said purchasing meals from restaurants, takeout, and delivery places makes it easier for families with children to manage their day-to-day lives;
- 52 percent of adults said they are likely to make a restaurant choice based on how much a restaurant supports charitable activities and the local community;
- 27 percent of adults said they are paying more attention to coupons and value specials when choosing their restaurants than they were two years ago.

According to a June 2009 poll published in *QSR Magazine:*

- Seventy percent of fast-food customers say their mood influences their decision to eat fast food;
- 59 percent say convenience does;
- 55 percent say cost does;
- 53 percent say menu offerings do;
- 50 percent say location does; and
- 24 percent say payment options do.
- Fifty-seven percent of fast-food customers are most likely to eat lunch at a fast-food restaurant;
- 27 percent are most likely to eat dinner there; and
- 8 percent are most likely to eat breakfast there.

Organizations to Contact

The editors have compiled the following list of organizations concerned with the issues debated in this book. The descriptions are derived from materials provided by the organizations. All have publications or information available for interested readers. The list was compiled on the date of publication of the present volume; the information provided here may change. Be aware that many organizations take several weeks or longer to respond to inquiries, so allow as much time as possible for the receipt of requested materials.

American Diabetes Association (ADA)
1701 N. Beauregard St.
Alexandria, VA 22311
(800) 342-2383
e-mail: askADA@diabetes.org
Web site: www.diabetes.org

The ADA, a not-for-profit health advocacy organization, works to prevent and cure diabetes, an obesity-related disease. Since food and good nutrition are critical to managing diabetes, the ADA educates people about changing their lifestyle and about disease prevention. As a part of its program, the ADA provides a guide to eating out and tips for how to order healthier items while dining at restaurants and fast-food establishments.

American Obesity Association (AOA)
8630 Fenton St., Ste. 814
Silver Spring, MD 20910
(301) 563-6526
Web site: www.obesity.org

The AOA is the leading scientific organization dedicated to the study of obesity and its health effects. Its researchers seek to understand the causes and treatment of obesity while also keeping the medical community informed of the latest advances in research. It publishes the journal *Obesity*, and several newsletters and reports found on its Web site discuss the effects of fast food on obesity.

Center for Science in the Public Interest (CSPI)
1875 Connecticut Ave. NW, Ste. 300
Washington, DC 20009-5728
(202) 332-9110
e-mail: cspi@cspinet.org
Web site: www.cspinet.org

Formed in 1971, the CSPI is a nonprofit education and consumer advocacy organization dedicated to fighting for government food policies and corporate practices that promote healthy diets. CSPI also works to prevent deceptive marketing practices and ensures that science is used for public welfare. It publishes *Nutrition Action Healthletter*, the most widely circulated health newsletter in North America.

Centers for Disease Control and Prevention (CDC)
Division of Nutrition and Physical Activity (DNPA)
1600 Clifton Rd.
Atlanta, GA 30333
(800) 232-4636
e-mail: cdcinfo@cdc.gov
Web site: www.cdc.gov/nccdphp/dnpa

The CDC is part of the National Institutes of Health (NIH), Department of Health and Human Services (DHHS). Its Division of Nutrition and Physical Activity has three focus areas: nutrition, physical activity, and obesity. The DNPA addresses the role of nutrition and physical activity in improving the public's health. DNPA activities include health promotion, research, training, and education. The DNPA maintains an archive of articles on its site, many of which are about the relationship between obesity and fast food.

The Council of Better Business Bureaus' Children's Food and Beverage Advertising Initiative
4200 Wilson Blvd., Ste. 800
Arlington, VA 22203-1838

(703) 276-0100

Web site: www.bbb.org/us/about-children-food-beverage-advertis ing-initiative

The Children's Food and Beverage Advertising Initiative was launched by the Council of Better Business Bureaus (BBB) in November 2006 to provide companies that advertise food and beverages to children with a transparent and accountable advertising regulation tool. The mission of the initiative is to shift the direction of advertisements directed to children under twelve to encourage healthier dietary choices. Participating companies must have standards consistent with U.S. Department of Agriculture and other scientific and government organizations and all companies that register with the initiative are monitored by the BBB to ensure compliance.

Food and Drug Administration (FDA)
5600 Fishers Ln.
Rockville, MD 20857
(888) 463-6332
e-mail: webmail@oc.fda.gov
Web site: www.fda.gov

The FDA is a public health agency charged with protecting American consumers by enforcing the Federal Food, Drug, and Cosmetic Act and several related public health laws. The FDA sends investigators and inspectors into the field to ensure that the country's almost ninety-five thousand FDA-regulated businesses are compliant. Its publications include government documents, reports, fact sheets, and press announcements. It also provides food labeling guidance and regulatory information for restaurants on its Web site.

Food Marketing Institute (FMI)
2345 Crystal Dr., Ste. 800
Arlington, VA 22202
(202) 452.8444
Web site: www.fmi.org

The FMI conducts programs in public affairs, food safety, research and education, and industry relations on behalf of food retailers and wholesalers in the United States and around the globe. By pursuing these activities, the FMI provides leadership and advocacy for the food distribution industry as it innovates to meet customers' changing needs. The Health and Wellness section on its Web site provides information about nutrition, nutrition labeling, and obesity.

Food Research and Action Center (FRAC)
1875 Connecticut Ave. NW, Ste. 540
Washington, DC 20009
(202) 986-2200
Web site: www.frac.org

FRAC is the leading national nonprofit organization working to improve public policies and public-private partnerships to eradicate hunger and undernutrition in the United States. FRAC serves as a watchdog of regulations and policies affecting the poor. It conducts public information campaigns, including the Campaign to End Childhood Hunger, to ensure that children of low-income families receive healthy and nutritious food so that they are able to learn and grow.

National Council of Chain Restaurants (NCCR)
325 Seventh St. NW, Ste. 1100
Washington, DC 20004
(202) 626-8189
e-mail: grannisk@nrf.com
Web site: www.nccr.net

The NCCR is the national trade association representing the chain restaurant industry and their 125,000 facilities. NCCR works to advance sound public policy that best serves the interests of chain restaurants and the 3 million people they employ. Its Web site provides up-to-date industry news, links to a number of government-relations resources, a Legislative Action Center where viewers can research legislation and learn how to work with Congress and, for members of the site, access to *NCCR Highlights Newsletter.*

National Restaurant Association
1200 Seventeenth St. NW
Washington, DC 20036
(202) 331-5900

e-mail: webchef@restaurant.org
Web site: www.restaurant.org

The National Restaurant Association represents, educates, and promotes America's $566 billion restaurant business. It promotes a pro-restaurant agenda, argues on behalf of the restaurant industry before Congress and federal regulatory agencies, and works to battle anti-restaurant initiatives. Reports, publications, press releases, and research about important topics affecting the food industry can all be found on its Web site, including the *2009 Restaurant Industry Forecast.*

United States Department of Agriculture (USDA)
Food and Nutrition Service (FNS)
1400 Independence Ave. SW
Washington, DC 20250
(202) 720-2791
Web site: www.usda.gov

The FNS is an agency of the USDA that is responsible for administering the nation's domestic nutrition assistance programs. It provides prepared meals, food assistance, and nutrition education materials to one in five Americans. The agency also encourages children and teens to follow the healthy eating guidelines set by MyPyramid in its "Eat Smart, Play Hard" campaign.

For Further Reading

Books

Critser, Greg. *Fat Land: How Americans Became the Fattest People in the World.* Boston: Mariner, 2004. An analysis of the social and economic factors that have led America to become a nation of obese people, including how the marketing tactics of fast-food restaurants have contributed to the population's weight gain.

Hughes, Siaron. *Chicken: Low Art, High Calorie.* New York: Mark Batty, 2009. A cultural examination of the branding methods of the fast-food industry, including signage, slogans, menus, and other visual elements found in fast-food chicken restaurants in London, England.

Participant Media. *Food, Inc.: A Participant Guide: How Industrial Food Is Making Us Sicker, Fatter, and Poorer—and What You Can Do About It.* Ed. Karl Weber. New York: Public Affairs, 2009. A companion book to the popular documentary, *Food, Inc.,* this collection of essays examines and challenges the corporate food industry.

Pollan, Michael. *The Omnivore's Dilemma: A Natural History of Four Meals.* New York: Penguin, 2007. Explores where food comes from by investigating the history of four meals, including tracing a meal at McDonald's back to its original ingredients.

Ritzer, George. *The McDonaldization of Society 5.* Los Angeles: Pine Forge, 2007. An analysis of how fast-food business practices have permeated all aspects of American society.

Schlosser, Eric. *Fast Food Nation.* New York: Harper Perennial, 2005. Argues that the fast-food industry has destroyed the American diet while simultaneously undermining the economy, the workforce, and American values.

Spurlock, Morgan. *Don't Eat This Book: Fast Food and the Supersizing of America.* New York: Berkeley Trade, 2006. A companion piece to the author's documentary, *Super Size Me,* this book explores the fast-food industry in great detail, particularly the impact of marketing directed toward children and young adults.

Talwar, Jennifer Parker. *Fast Food, Fast Track: Immigrants, Big Business, and the American Dream.* Boulder, CO: Westview, 2002. Discusses how fast-food restaurants offer employment opportunities for newly-arrived immigrants in America.

Periodicals and Internet Sources

Aarons, Barry M. "Which Is Worse: Big Mac or Big Brother?" *Human Events,* July 12, 2006.

Beato, Greg. "Where's the Beef? Thank McDonald's for Keeping You Thin," *Reason,* January 2008. www.reason.com/news/show/123473.html.

Davis, Brennan, and Christopher Carpenter, "Proximity of Fast-Food Restaurants to Schools and Adolescent Obesity," *American Journal of Public Health*, vol. 99, no. 3, March 2009.

Duffy, Emmett. "Fast Food: On the Fast Track to Environmental Ruin," Natural Patriot, December 5, 2008. http://naturalpatriot.org/2008/12/05/fast-food-on-the-fast-track-to-environmental-ruin.

Economist. "Waist Banned," July 30, 2009. www.economist.com/businessfinance/displaystory.cfm?story_id=14120903.

Engelhard, Carolyn L., Arthur Garson Jr., and Stan Dorn. "Reducing Obesity: Policy Strategies from the Tobacco Wars," Urban Institute, July 2009. www.urban.org/uploadedpdf/411926_reducing_obesity.pdf.

Gervitz, Leslie. "School Near Fast Food Joint? Expect Fatter Kids," Reuters, March 13, 2009.

Gregory, Sean. "Fast Food: Would You Like 1,000 Calories with That?" *Time*, June 29, 2009.

Gunlock, Julie. "Eating Is No Fun Anymore," *National Review*, August 7, 2009.

Gupta, Arun. "How We Became a Society of Gluttonous Junk Food Addicts," AlterNet.org, August 5, 2009. www.alternet.org/healthwellness/141776/how_we_became_a_society_of_gluttonous_junk_food_addicts/?page=entire.

Hirsch, Jerry. "Study Links Student Obesity to Distance from Fast Food: Low-Cost, High-Cal Eateries Near Schools Increase the Odds, Researchers Say," *Los Angeles Times*, March 23, 2009.

Kiley, David. "Fast Food Menu Calorie Counter Should Be National Law," *BusinessWeek,* July 17, 2009.

Miller, Thomas P. "Should We Fight Today's War on Obesity like the Last War on Tobacco?" *American,* August 7, 2009.

Minkin, Tracy, and Brittani Renaud. "Fast Food: Not Always Unhealthy?" ABCNews.com, March 9, 2009. http://abcnews .com/m/screen?id=7026816&pid=26.

Neil, Dan. "Seduced by a Burger: Carl's Jr. Advertising Finds Its Groove," *Los Angeles Times,* April 14, 2009.

Niles, Meredith. "Burger King Launches Film *Whopper Virgins,* Simplifies U.S. to Land of Fast Food," Grist, January 8, 2009. www.grist.org/article/If-they-have-it-their-way-theyll-supersize-the-world.

O'Hagan, Andrew. "Junk Food Should Be Taxed Like Booze," *Telegraph* (London), October 11, 2006.

Parikh, Rahul K. "Indiana Jones and the Kingdom of Fat Kids," *Slate,* May 21, 2008. www.salon.com/mwt/vital_signs/2008/05/21/ indiana_jones_obesity/index.html.

Rabin, Roni Caryn. "Proximity to Fast Food a Factor in Student Obesity," *New York Times,* March 25, 2009.

Saletan, William. "Food Apartheid: Banning Fast Food in Poor Neighborhoods," *Slate,* July 31, 2008. www.slate.com/id/2196397.

Schaper, Donna, and Molly Schwartz. "Getting Real About Food," *Nation,* June 25, 2007.

Schor, Elana. "Los Angeles City Council Issues Fast-Food Ban for Poor Neighbourhoods," *Guardian,* (London), July 30, 2008.

Severson, Kim. "Los Angeles Stages a Fast Food Intervention," *New York Times,* August 12, 2008.

Soupcoff, Marni. "Food Apartheid," *Regulation,* Cato Institute, Fall 2008. www.cato.org/pubs/regulation/regv31n3/v31n3-final.pdf.

Sullum, Jacob. "Are You Sure You Want Fries with That? Mandatory Calorie Counts Cross the Line Between Informing and Nagging," *Reason,* August 20, 2008. www.reason.com/news/show/128178 .html.

Web Sites

A Calorie Counter (www.acaloriecounter.com). A Calorie Counter is a free Web site that allows users to search the USDA food nutrition database. Entering any food item into the search bar brings up the full nutrition facts for that food, such as calories, protein, carbohydrates, fat, sugar, cholesterol, sodium, and vitamins. The site is intended to help people improve their diet, weight, and health by making them more aware of the nutrition contained in the foods they are eating. It contains a link to Fast Food Restaurants & Nutrition Facts Compared, which compares nutrition facts of the most popular foods from over twenty fast-food restaurants.

CalorieKing (www.calorieking.com). CalorieKing is a science-based Web site designed to educate, motivate, and inspire people to pursue the goal of lifelong weight control. It offers Web-based and clinical tools to help users understand the truth about food, and it encourages users to avoid negative advertising messages about food. An extensive food database helps users understand the caloric values of the food consumed every day.

FastFood.com (www.fastfood.com). FastFood.com is a Web site that offers a comprehensive guide to the fast-food industry. It has a database containing information on hundreds of thousands of restaurants, including fast-food chains such as McDonald's, Taco Bell, and Subway. Nutritional information, including fat and calorie counts for meals, can also be determined by using the site's calorie counter.

Slow Food (www.slowfood.com). Founded in 1989, Slow Food is a member-supported nonprofit organization dedicated to counteracting fast food and fast lifestyles, the disappearance of local food traditions, and the lack of interest people have in the food they consume. Slow Food seeks to protect the biodiversity of the world's food supply due to the onslaught of convenience and industrial agribusiness. The Web site contains links to the Slow Food & Terra Madre Newsletter, the *Slow Food Almanac 2008*, and national newsletters from countries around the world.

Index

should not profit from bad
behavior, 69–70

H
Hamlin, Amie, 53
Hanrahan, Karen, 13
Hardee's
    Monster Thickburger, 28,
    28
Haskell, Dean, 20
Health-care system, 26
Heiderscheidt, Rachel, 9
Hill, James, 33
Hoyte, Arthur, 43

I
Ingredients
    in Big Mac secret sauce,
    16–17
    of fast foods, 81–82
*International Journal of
    Behavioral Nutrition and
    Physical Activity,* 98
International Journal of Obesity,
    35
International Stroke
    Conference, 38
Irani, Sarah, 12

J
Jacobson, Michael, 44
Journal of Law & Economics, 88,
    91

K
Kaiser Family Foundation, 63

Kentucky Fried Chicken (KFC),
    44–45
    Double Down, 28–30
    Famous Bowl, 27
Kilpatrick, Kwame, 68, 71
Krispy Kreme, 26

L
Lancet (journal), 55
Lederhausen, Mats, 22
Los Angeles, 55, 57, 60
Lyons, Rob, 79

M
Maine, 74–75
    junk food tax in, 68
Markels, Alex, 19
McConnell, Mitch, 39
McDonald's, 82
    amount of beef processed
    by, 15
    lawsuits against, 7–8, 38
    menu for diabetics, 45
    posting of nutritional
    information by, *75*
    Ronald McDonald, use of
    as marketing tool by,
    72
Milosheff, Peter, 49
Mnaymneh, Sami, 51
Moran, Monty, 23
Morford, Mark, 85

N
National Bureau of Economic
    Research (NBER), 96

Picture Credits

Maury Aaseng, 14, 21, 29, 34, 46, 51, 59, 65, 77, 93, 99

AP Images, 23, 28, 64, 70, 75

Carlos Barria/Reuters/Landov, 48

Mike Blake/Reuters/Landov, 81

© Bubbles Photolibrary/Alamy, 92

Ben Hider/Getty Images, 72

© John Powell Photographer/Alamy, 17

Saeed Khan/AF Getty Images, 97

Phil McCarten/Reuters/Landov, 58

© Shruti Moghe/Alamy, 33

Finbarr O'Reilly/Reuters/Landov, 39

Steve Parsons/PA Photos Landov, 11

Reuters/Finbarr O'Reilly/Landov, 54

Shannon Stapleton/Reuters/Landov, 44

UPI/Landov, 87